THE *Pennington* COOKBOOK

THE Pennington COOKBOOK

The Art of Taste, The Science of Nutrition

CHEF KELLY PATRICK WILLIAMS

Enjoy the book and eating well.
Kelly Patrick Williams

PELICAN PUBLISHING COMPANY
Gretna 2000

Copyright © 2000
By Kelly Patrick Williams

*The word "Pelican" and the depiction of a pelican are trademarks
of Pelican Publishing, Inc. and are registered in the
U.S. Patent and Trademark Office.*

All rights reserved. No part of this book may be reproduced or used in any form or by any means, electronic or mechanical, including photocopying, recording, or by an information retrieval system, without permission in writing from the author and the publisher.

Library of Congress Cataloging-in-Publication Data

Williams, Kelly Patrick.
   The Pennington cookbook / Kelly Patrick Williams ; preface by George A. Bray.
      p. cm—(Studies in social medicine)
   Includes index.
   ISBN 1-56554-679-2 (alk. paper)
   1. Cookery. 2. Low-fat die—Recipes. 3. Nutrition. I. Title II. Series.
TX714.W5236 2000
641.5'638—dc21
                                                                                     99-056380

Manufactured in the United States of America
Published by Pelican Publishing Company, Inc.
1000 Burmaster Street, Gretna, Louisiana 70053

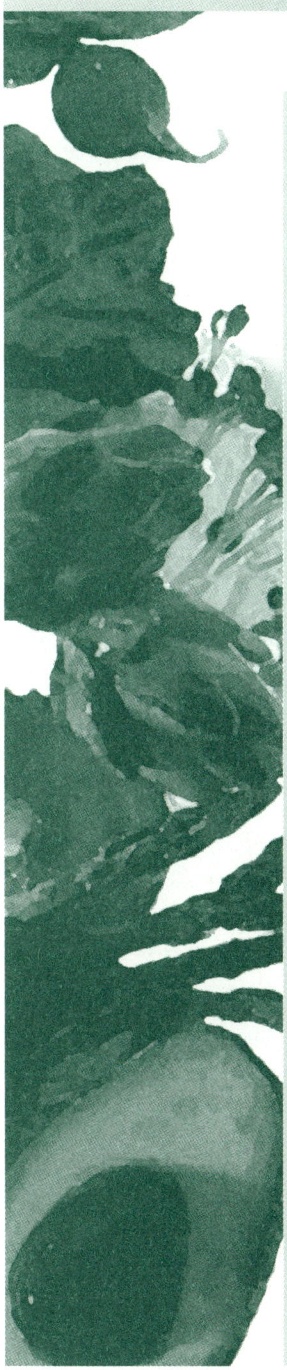

CONTENTS

Preface   7

Introduction   9

Chapter 1
Appetizers and Hors d'Oeuvres   13

Chapter 2
Breakfast and Brunch   29

Chapter 3
Salads and Sandwiches   39

Chapter 4
Soups and Stews   57

Chapter 5
Vegetarian   71

Chapter 6
Chicken and Poultry   85

Chapter 7
Fish and Seafood   101

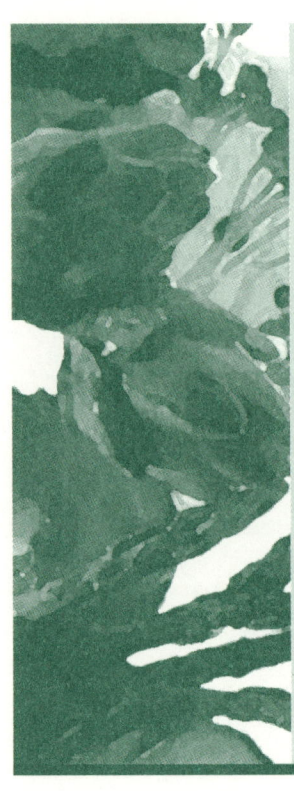

Chapter 8
Meats of All Kinds   127

Chapter 9
Sauces, Dressings, and Garnishes   143

Chapter 10
Rice, Potatoes, and Sides   155

Chapter 11
Desserts and Sweets   167

Index   179

Preface

The recipes in *The Pennington Cookbook* represent a tasty approach to healthier eating and living. We should strive to eat a diet that is low in fat, particularly saturated fat, high in fruits and vegetables, limited in salt, and drink alcohol only in moderation. This can be achieved through variety and moderation. Variety is the spice of life when it comes to nutrition and health. No one food gives us the wide range of nutrients our bodies need. I recommend to all my friends and patients that they eat many different foods and enjoy all foods in moderation. This collection is very much in keeping with that philosophy and makes it possible to maintain a diet that is balanced in nutrients, low in fat, and high in flavor.

The Pennington Cookbook also reflects the Pennington Biomedical Research Center's focus on the role that the food we eat plays in our health and quality of life. Since the Pennington Center opened in 1988, we have pursued a mission of healthier lives through nutrition and preventive medicine. Our founders, "Doc" and Irene Pennington and their family, believed that the food we eat has a profound effect on our health. Their $125-million gift to Louisiana State University led to the construction of a core research complex that spans 223,000 square feet—an area the size of five football fields. The later addition of a 96,000-square-foot conference and education center now complements the research complex.

Today, forty basic laboratories, inpatient and outpatient clinics, the finest research kitchen in the world, and more than $15 million in technologically advanced equipment are devoted to understanding the link between nutrition and our health. With a staff of more than 350 physicians, scientists, and support personnel and an operating budget approaching $20 million a year, the Pennington Center is poised to play a leading role in nutritional research for decades to come.

While much of the Pennington Center's scientific interests are rooted in the laboratory and the clinic, Kelly Patrick Williams' work is an example of our efforts to bring the results of our research into the kitchen and the home. I believe a healthy diet shouldn't be a fad, but should be embraced as a lifestyle. If your diet isn't something you enjoy and appreciate, you won't stick with it for long.

Because there is no sacrifice involved, Kelly's approach to cooking makes healthy eating easy. As you prepare these dishes, I'm sure you'll agree that "bland" isn't a word that comes to mind when describing Kelly's recipes. You aren't giving up anything that isn't returned in the form of flavors and aromas you may have missed with more traditional approaches to cooking.

Each of these recipes is a reflection of Kelly's experiences at the Pennington Center. Her position provides a unique appreciation for cooking and health. A gourmet chef trained at The Culinary Institute in Hyde Park, New York, Kelly came to the Pennington Center from Southern California, where she cooked in several outstanding restaurants.

Kelly's position at the Pennington Center was established because of our wish to combine the culinary talents of a chef with the expertise of the many registered dietitians that we have on staff. It was our belief that dietitians offer the nutritional foundation for healthy eating, while a gourmet chef brings to the table creativity and an understanding of the interaction between foods and flavors. The result is the best of both worlds—dishes and meals that are healthy and taste wonderful.

With that philosophy in mind, Kelly has worked with our dietitians on a wide range of research projects. For example, through a contract with the U.S. Army Research Institute of Environmental Medicine, she helped design and test low-fat, low-cholesterol, and low-sodium but tasty recipes that are now served to our nation's armed services personnel. Kelly also joined with our dietitians to teach cooks in school cafeteria kitchens techniques for healthier cooking through a grant from the U.S. Department of Agriculture. That's not to mention the numerous other research projects she has collaborated on and the parties, dinners, and banquets she has either catered or organized for the Pennington Center.

Along the way, Kelly became the host of *Savor the Regions,* a cooking show produced by Louisiana Public Broadcasting and sponsored by the Pennington Biomedical Research Center Foundation and Lake Charles Memorial Hospital. The show, which can be seen on many Public Broadcasting Service stations across the country, explores cuisines from around the nation and the world and demonstrates how these recipes can be prepared in a manner that is "gourmet without the guilt."

As you can see, Kelly has a background that few chefs can match. You hold in your hands the fruits of those experiences. Enjoy.

George A. Bray, M.D.
Executive Director Emeritus
and Boyd Professor
Pennington Biomedical
Research Center

Introduction

The recipes in this book represent the journey I have taken while working with the Pennington Biomedical Research Center in its quest to promote healthier lives through research. The food reflects the personality of the cuisine that I discovered to be the most full-flavored I have seen in nutritional foods.

When I came to Pennington from California, where I worked in the restaurant and hotel industry, I arrogantly believed that I understood what "healthy" food was. I, of course, was living in California and reverently read every health and fitness magazine known to man. I also arrogantly believed that I understood what most people did and did not enjoy eating, having fed and entertained so many people throughout my cooking career.

Well, I had a lot to learn, and Pennington soon threw me into the real world. Within the first month, I was sent on my first study for the United States Army. Later, I traveled from state to state working with American school food service. Daily, I work with very talented nutritionists on research studies to prepare foods that the average person will eat and enjoy. Our goal is to gain knowledge concerning high blood pressure, heart disease, and diabetes.

The foods are not created for one big night on the town, but for daily life. I deal with people from every walk of life, not just those who appreciate fine and expensive cuisine. What a fantastic and incredible challenge for a chef to use a knowledge of food and all the intricate qualities of various cuisine to inspire full-flavored and exciting foods for everyday life—foods that must meet specific nutritional standards, but, most importantly, that everyone must enjoy, not just the privileged few. It has been a never-ending journey, and this book represents all the discoveries made along the way.

My journey with Pennington has not always been devoted to institutional foods. Somewhere along the way, I started speaking to people on a more personal level. I was determined to make the message of promoting a healthy life one that did not include sacrificing the things people love, but did include making healthy food part of their lives. So many times I see people sacrifice good flavor and quality in the foods they eat because good food does not fit into their daily schedule.

When I say good food, I mean food that makes you feel good and tastes great. These foods may be part of an elegant dinner you prepare for your closest friends, or the meal you prepare in twenty minutes for the family as soon as you get off work. Some of the recipes are made to inspire you to learn about new styles of food and ingredients. Just as I am in a never-ending learning process, I hope you will also challenge your palate to enjoy new flavors. I hope to inspire people to make some healthier foods part of their personal list of comfort foods. Therefore, you will find many hearty and simple dishes throughout the book as well.

As previously noted, the recipes in this book are designed for everyday use by everyone. This book is not intended as a guide for drastic weight loss or for pre-existing health conditions, although your doctor might recommend it for such reasons. Some recipes are higher in fat or in sodium. The reason is that the author is a chef. It has been written for the sake of flavor first and nutrition a very close second. If a recipe was fantastic but needed just a tiny bit more olive oil to enhance the flavor, the adjustment was made despite the fact that it would be a little over the recommended values.

I promote a healthy life full of good food. Don't be too preoccupied with the nutritional analysis of one dish. One dish is only part of one meal, which is part of a whole day, part of a week, a month, a year, a whole life. By keeping this in mind and living a healthy life, you can have an extra spring in your step and a glow on your face.

I want to leave you with one final note. If this book can do anything, I hope it inspires you to try at least a few of the recipes with friends and family and get into the kitchen more often. I hope you enjoy preparing the foods as much as those who will enjoy eating them.

I understand that our lives are very busy today. The most frequent request I receive from people is for me to cook the food and drop it by around 7 P.M.! But I believe in cooking for health and the importance of scheduling our lives to take time for meals. Imagine an ideal family dinner. As people begin to gather, one person is placing ice in the glasses while another sets the table. The finishing touches are made on dinner and it is brought to the table. While each person describes the events of his or her day, the delicious food is enjoyed by all.

Different people then help gather the dishes to bring them to the sink, laughing about who will scour the last pot. As the meal comes to a close, everyone returns to his or her personal business. Now that's healthy eating.

THE Pennington COOKBOOK

CHAPTER 1

Appetizers and Hors d'Oeuvres

Avocado and Citrus Canapé
Barbecued Oysters
Black Bean Tart with Chili Crust
Brie and Pear Torte
Caviar Crisps
Crab-Stuffed Artichoke
Grilled Shrimp Baha Rolls
Grilled Zucchini Spears
Kale and Tasso Pastries
Lemon Herb Dip
Louisiana Lump Crabmeat Dip
Mediterranean Hummus
Orange Ginger Chicken Sate
Oysters Louisiane
Pears with Walnut Cheese
Poor Man's Caviar with Italian Herbed Crackers
Smoked Salmon and Endive Canapé
Spicy Ancho Dip
Sun-Dried Tomato-Stuffed Mushrooms
Warm Spinach and Artichoke Dip
Wild Mushroom Torte

Avocado and Citrus Canapé

1 package whole wheat crackers
2 avocados
1 grapefruit
1 orange
2 jalapeno peppers, thinly sliced

This is a quick hors d'oeuvre that can be put together in minutes for guests who might happen to drop by.
Serves 12

Remove the skin and pit from the avocados. With a knife, cut the skins from the grapefruit and orange, removing any white pith, Cut out each section of fruit. Add any juices on your cutting board to the avocados. Mash avocados and juices with the back of a fork. Soak slices of jalapeno in cold water for 10 minutes, then drain. To assemble, place a large tbsp. of avocado on a cracker, top with a citrus section and then a pepper slice.

Calories (kcal)	76
Total Fat (gm)	5
% Calories from Fat	55%
Cholesterol (mg)	0
Sodium (mg)	4

Barbecued Oysters

2 doz. oysters, shucked
1 cup Roasted Pepper Barbecue Sauce, recipe found in book

Prepare these indoors or out. Serve on a platter over rock salt and garnished with chives.
Serves 12

Preheat broiler or barbecue pit. For a broiler, shuck the oysters. Place each shucked oyster in an oyster shell or small ramekin. Top with 1 tsp. of barbecue sauce. Broil for 4 minutes. For a barbecue pit, place whole oysters on a hot barbecue pit, unshucked, with the flatter side of the oyster faced up. When the oyster is almost done, the shell will unseal itself. Carefully remove from the pit with a towel or hot pads. With an oyster knife or dull kitchen knife, pry the top of the shell off. It will remove much easier than if it were uncooked.

Calories (kcal)	16
Total Fat (gm)	0
% Calories from Fat	22%
Cholesterol (mg)	0
Sodium (mg)	170

Place a tsp. of barbecue sauce on top of oyster and return to the barbecue pit for 1 minute. Both methods make delicious oysters, but an added smoky grilled flavor comes with the barbecue pit method.

Black Bean Tart with Chili Crust

- 2 cups saltine crackers, crumbled fine
- 2 tbsp. unsalted butter, melted
- 2 dried Anaheim or Ancho chilies, ground
- 3 egg whites
- 1 cup onion, chopped
- 2 tbsp. garlic, chopped
- 3 cans black beans, rinsed and drained
- 2 roasted red peppers
- ¼ cup sun-dried tomatoes, chopped
- ½ cup warm water
- 1 cup fat-free sour cream
- 2 limes
- ¼ tsp. cloves
- 2 tbsp. chives, chopped

The chili crust is what makes this so very special. If dried peppers are not available, substitute with chili powder or paprika. Serves 12

Pulverize the crackers very fine in a food processor. Remove to a bowl, and blend with the melted butter, ground peppers, and egg whites. Press into the bottom of a 10-inch tart pan or an 8-inch spring form pan. In a medium sauté pan, sauté the onion and garlic. Add the rinsed and drained black beans and water.

Cook for 5-10 minutes, or until thick creamy. Hydrate the sun-dried tomatoes in warm water for 5 minutes. Roast the red bell peppers, skin and seed. Puree the roasted red bell peppers and sun-dried tomatoes in a food processor. In a bowl, whip the sour cream with the lime and clove.

To assemble the tart, spread the black beans on the chili crust, layer roasted pepper and tomato on top. Spread sour cream on top of pepper mixture. Bake in a 350-degree oven for 20 minutes. Sprinkle with chives and serve.

Calories (kcal)	396
Total Fat (gm)	7
% Calories from Fat	17%
Cholesterol (mg)	9
Sodium (mg)	631

Brie and Pear Torte

6 oz. Brie round
2 pears
3 slices sourdough bread
1 cup balsamic vinegar

Calories (kcal)	86
Total Fat (gm)	4
% Calories from Fat	43%
Cholesterol (mg)	14
Sodium (mg)	131

A delightful and easy appetizer. Be as creative as you would like with this dish. You can use different styles of bread, such as caraway loaf or an olive loaf. Camembert or goat's cheese may also be substituted for the Brie. If calories allow, garnish with toasted walnuts or almonds.
Serves 12

Slice the small Brie round laterally in half like you would a cake round. Peel, core, and slice the pears. Cut the bread slices into rounds the same size as the Brie round. Place balsamic vinegar in a small pan on the stove and reduce by half. To assemble, lay a round of bread on a serving plate, topped with a Brie round, another slice of bread, followed by pear slices. Drizzle with balsamic reduction. Finish with a Brie round, final bread round, and pear slices, and finally drizzle with remaining balsamic reduction.

Caviar Crisps

24 potato chips, unsalted
1 pint fat-free sour cream
2 tbsp. lemon juice
3 tbsp. chives, chopped
1 jar caviar

Depending on the caviar used for this hors d'oeuvre, this dish can be as extravagant as you wish.
Serves 12

Blend the sour cream, lemon juice, and chives together. Place a tsp. of sour cream on each potato chip, followed by ½ tsp. of caviar.

Calories (kcal)	65
Total Fat (gm)	2
% Calories from Fat	25%
Cholesterol (mg)	15
Sodium (mg)	74

Crab-Stuffed Artichoke

1 artichokes, large
2 lemons
2 bay leaves
3 tbsp. salt
1 tabasco pepper
3 cups water
1 tbsp. olive oil
1 cup onion, minced
2 tbsp. garlic, minced
½ cup celery, chopped
½ cup bell pepper, chopped
¼ cup red bell pepper
1 cup white wine
1½ cups crab meat
1 cup bread crumbs
1 tsp. salt

A great tailgating appetizer or picnic snack.
Serves 6

Steam the large artichoke in the water, seasoned with 1 lemon, bay, pepper, and salt. After 10 minutes, remove and allow to cool, reserving steaming liquid in pan. In a medium sauté pan, heat olive oil, and sauté the onion, garlic, celery, bell pepper, and red bell pepper. Add white wine and cook 2 minutes. Remove from heat and fold in crab meat and bread crumbs, and moisten with chicken stock to the right consistency.

From the top middle of the artichoke, remove the center leaves, and carefully remove the choke. Stuff the middle with stuffing, then place 2 tsp. of stuffing in between the leaves. Place stuffed artichoke back in the steamer and steam for another 10 minutes.

Calories (kcal)	190
Total Fat (gm)	4
% Calories from Fat	21%
Cholesterol (mg)	26
Sodium (mg)	625

Grilled Shrimp Baha Rolls

1 doz. 10-inch flour tortillas
½ cup avocado, sliced
1 cup romaine lettuce, shaved
3 carrots, julienne and blanch
½ red bell pepper
½ lb. medium shrimp, peeled
1 tbsp. paprika
2 tbsp. lime juice
1 tsp. kosher salt
1½ cups tomato, chopped
1 tbsp. cilantro, chopped

Serve on lined platters on an hors d'oeuvre table. Also a great luncheon item.
Serves 6

Prepare an outdoor grill, or heat a broiler. In a medium bowl, combine the shrimp, lime juice, paprika, and salt. Grill 1 minute on each side, or until cooked through. Combine the tomato and cilantro in a bowl. Season with salt and pepper. Lay a tortilla on a clean, flat surface. Place some lettuce, avocado, carrot, red bell pepper, and shrimp down the center of the tortilla in a stripping fashion, leaving a 2-inch lip free at the top and bottom. Roll up jelly-roll fashion or like a sushi roll. Secure with toothpicks down the center. Cut in between each toothpick, and flip onto its side, exposing the fillings. Serve with seasoned tomatoes.

Calories (kcal)	322
Total Fat (gm)	8
% Calories from Fat	23%
Cholesterol (mg)	58
Sodium (mg)	722

Grilled Zucchini Spears

4 zucchini
3 oz. prosciutto, thinly sliced
Cracked black pepper

Have your butcher slice the prosciutto paper thin. If the ham is not cut thinly, it will not "break" to the tooth. For a variation, substitute the zucchini for blanched green beans or asparagus spears.
Serves 12

Cut zucchini into 2-3-inch spears. Cut thinly sliced ham into strips and decoratively wrap around zucchini like a barbershop pole. Grill on an outdoor or indoor grill for 2 minutes or until moisture begins to emit from squash. Season with fresh cracked black pepper and serve.

Calories (kcal)	20
Total Fat (gm)	1
% Calories from Fat	28%
Cholesterol (mg)	5
Sodium (mg)	192

Appetizers and Hors d'Oeuvres

Kale and Tasso Pastries

½ lb. red potatoes
1 tbsp. canola oil
½ cup onion, chopped
1 tbsp. garlic, chopped
1 lb. kale, washed and deveined, chopped
3 tbsp. tasso ham, minced
½ cup part-skim ricotta cheese
Salt and pepper, to taste
10 sheets filo dough
Vegetable cooking spray

These savory little pastries are great hors d'oeuvres, but also a great accompaniment as a side dish with practically any menu. If tasso ham is not available, substitute with prosciutto.
Serves 12

Quarter the potatoes and steam until tender. Allow to cool. Place in a mixer and mash smooth. Heat a sauté pan with canola oil. Sauté the onion and garlic. Add the tasso ham. Cook 2 minutes before adding the kale. Turn the kale in the pan until wilted. Remove from heat. Blend the potato, ricotta, and kale mixture.

On a clean working space, lay one sheet of filo dough with the long side facing you. Spray with cooking spray and top with a second sheet of dough. Cut crosswise into 5 strips. Spoon 2 tsp. of filling on the bottom edge of a strip. Fold the corner over filling to form a triangle. Continue folding to maintain triangular shape. Repeat with the rest of the dough and the filling. Everything up to this point may be done a day in advance. Bake triangles in a 400-degree oven for 10 minutes.

Calories (kcal)	111
Total Fat (gm)	3
% Calories from Fat	27%
Cholesterol (mg)	5
Sodium (mg)	160

Lemon Herb Dip

1 cup fat-free mayonnaise
1 cup buttermilk
1 tbsp. honey
Pinch cayenne pepper
1 tbsp. basil, chopped
½ tbsp. sage, chopped
½ tbsp. thyme, chopped
1 tbsp. chives, chopped
1 tbsp. dill, chopped
3 lemons
1 tsp. salt
1 tbsp. canola oil

*Serve with an assortment of vegetable crudite and crackers.
Serves 12*

Zest your lemons. Heat canola oil with zest and mixed chopped herbs for 2 minutes. Whip with mayonnaise and buttermilk and the juice from the zested lemons. Season further with cayenne and salt.

Calories (kcal)	322
Total Fat (gm)	8
% Calories from Fat	23%
Cholesterol (mg)	58
Sodium (mg)	722

Louisiana Lump Crabmeat Dip

1 cup fat-free cream cheese, room temperature
1 cup light mayonnaise
1 cup green onion, thinly sliced
½ tsp. garlic powder
1 tsp. Tabasco sauce
1 lb. fresh lump crabmeat, drained
1/4 tsp. paprika

*A simple dip for casual tailgating or an elegant cocktail party.
Serve with melba toast or any herb baked cracker (see page 23).
Serves 12*

In a mixer, blend the cheese, mayonnaise, onion, garlic, and Tabasco. Turn off mixer and fold in crabmeat. Cover and chill. Sprinkle with paprika and serve with melba toasts.

Calories (kcal)	100
Total Fat (gm)	5
% Calories from Fat	41%
Cholesterol (mg)	38
Sodium (mg)	315

Appetizers and Hors d'Oeuvres

Mediterranean Hummus

1½ cups chickpeas, canned, rinse and drain
½ cup low-sodium chicken broth
2 tbsp. olive oil
1½ tbsp. fresh herbs
3 pita bread rounds, quartered

The fresh herbs add some dimension to a dish so low in fat. Use herbs such as rosemary, oregano, Italian parsley, basil, and some lemon zest. For a twist, use rinsed and drained white beans for a little different texture.
Serves 12

Rinse and drain the canned chickpeas, then puree in a food processor. Heat the olive oil in a sauté pan, add the chickpeas and the chicken broth. Cook for 3 minutes or until consistency is a smooth creamy texture. Fold in the fresh herbs. Serve with baked pita chips.

Calories (kcal)	98
Total Fat (gm)	3
% Calories from Fat	25%
Cholesterol (mg)	0
Sodium (mg)	192

Orange Ginger Chicken Sate

1½ lb. chicken tenders
2 tbsp. ginger root, minced
1 tbsp. garlic, minced
1 tsp. sesame oil
¼ cup rice wine vinegar
1 cup orange juice
3 tbsp. soy sauce
½ tsp. crushed red pepper
Bamboo skewers, soaked in water
¼ cup scallions, sliced at an angle
¼ cup orange sections

Chicken tenders have a thick, fibrous membrane that needs to be stripped from the meat; otherwise the meat may be chewy. This is done by scraping a chef knife along the tender while pulling the membrane . . . a lot like skinning a fish.
Serves 6

In a bowl, combine the ginger, garlic, sesame oil, rice wine vinegar, orange juice, soy sauce, and crushed red pepper. Fold the chicken in marinade and allow to sit for at least 2 hours. Skewer chicken on bamboo skewers. Heat a broiler or outdoor grill and cook skewers 2 minutes on each side. Garnish with scallions and orange sections.

Calories (kcal)	138
Total Fat (gm)	2
% Calories from Fat	13%
Cholesterol (mg)	53
Sodium (mg)	356

Oysters Louisiane

- 3 doz. oysters, scrubbed
- ½ tbsp. olive oil
- 2 tbsp. shallots, minced
- 2 tsp. garlic, minced
- ¼ cup artichoke hearts, chopped
- ¼ cup flour
- ½ cup evaporated skim milk
- 2 bunches fresh spinach, steamed
- 3 tbsp. basil, fresh, chopped
- 1 tsp. coarsely ground pepper
- 1 cup crab meat
- 3 tbsp. Pernod
- ¼ cup Romano cheese
- 2 cups rock salt

This is a wonderful appetizer taking ideas from Louisiana favorites Oysters Rockefeller and Oysters Bienville, combining them into a fabulous heart-healthy dish. The filling for the oysters maintains great flavor, even though very low in fat, by using a full flavored cheese—a little goes a long way.
Serves 6

Shuck the oysters carefully to free the oyster from the shell without tearing the meat. Discard the top shell, leaving the oyster sitting inside its bottom shell. Pour the rock salt into a gratin plate or a sheet pan, lay the oysters in the shell on the salt so as not to tip over, and place in the refrigerator. Heat olive oil in a sauté pan, and sauté the shallots and garlic. Add the chopped artichoke hearts, and sprinkle all ingredients with flour. Sauté 1 minute, then add the milk. Stirring constantly, bring to a slow simmer until sauce thickens. Do not boil or it will separate. Fold in the spinach, basil, pepper, crab meat, and Pernod. Place 2 tbsp. of filling on top of each oyster, then sprinkle with Romano cheese. Broil in the oven for 5 minutes or until the filling is bubbling and the cheese is melted.

Calories (kcal)	119
Total Fat (gm)	3
% Calories from Fat	27%
Cholesterol (mg)	29
Sodium (mg)	188

Pears with Walnut Cheese

- 4 pears, cored
- ½ cup feta cheese
- ¼ cup plain yogurt
- 2 tsp. lemon juice
- 3 tbsp. walnuts, chopped

An elegant passed hors d'oeuvre. The pears can also be used to dress up a green salad made with a walnut vinaigrette.
Serves 12

Cut pears into wedges and remove core. In a bowl, whip the feta, mayonnaise, and lemon juice. Spread one tbsp. of

Appetizers and Hors d'Oeuvres

Calories (kcal)	*48*
Total Fat (gm)	*2*
% Calories from Fat	*28%*
Cholesterol (mg)	*5*
Sodium (mg)	*55*

cheese on the end of each pear wedge. Roll or sprinkle walnuts over cheese to stick.

Poor Man's Caviar with Italian Herbed Crackers

2 cups eggplant, chopped
½ cup tomato, chopped
1 anchovy fillet, packed in salt
2 tsp. extra virgin olive oil
½ tsp. cracked black pepper
2 tbsp. capers, chopped
1 tbsp. balsamic vinegar
2 cups cornmeal
2 cups flour
¼ cup fresh herbs, chopped
2 egg whites
½ cup shortening
1 cup water

Also called Aubergine Caviar; the anchovies give this dish its full flavor. If you are pressed for time, omit the hand-made crackers and use store-bought, although you will be impressed by how easy it is to make your own.
Serves 12

Place eggplant on a sheet pan and roast in a 350-degree oven for 25 minutes. Allow to cool. In a food processor, combine the roasted eggplant, capers, olive oil, balsamic vinegar, and anchovy fillet. Process until combined. Place in a bowl, and fold in tomato and pepper. Let sit 20 minutes. Meanwhile, combine the cornmeal, flour, and herbs. Cut the shortening into flour mixture. Whip the egg whites with water. Place in a well made by the flour and shortening mixture and combine gradually. Roll out onto a floured work place. Bake in a 350-degree oven. Crack into irregularly shaped crackers and serve with Poor Man's Caviar.

Calories (kcal)	*252*
Total Fat (gm)	*10*
% Calories from Fat	*36%*
Cholesterol (mg)	*0*
Sodium (mg)	*39*

Smoked Salmon and Endive Canapé

- 2 heads endive
- 5 oz. smoked salmon, chopped
- 8 oz. non-fat cream cheese
- 1 tsp. lemon juice
- 2 tsp. coarsely ground pepper
- 1 cup red onion, thinly sliced
- ½ cup red wine vinegar
- ¼ cup sugar
- 3 tbsp. fresh dill

An elegant hors d'oeuvre for a special occasion. Purchase Belgian endive, which looks like a white and green torpedo. Many grocery stores refer to frisse lettuce as curly endive, which can be confusing and misleading for this recipe.
Serves 12

Divide the endive and trim to make individual "boat-shaped" lettuce leaves. In a mixer, whip the cream cheese, chopped salmon, lemon, and cracked black pepper. Heat the vinegar and sugar to a boil. Pour over onions and allow to sit 5 minutes. Remove from hot brine to chill. To assemble, spoon a tbsp. of salmon cream into endive spears or boats, top with pickled onion, and garnish with dill sprig.

Calories (kcal)	*70*
Total Fat (gm)	*1*
% Calories from Fat	*12%*
Cholesterol (mg)	*4*
Sodium (mg)	*215*

Spicy Ancho Dip

- 1 cup fat-free sour cream
- ½ cup fat-free mayonnaise
- ½ cup white wine
- 1 whole dried Anaheim or Ancho pepper, minced
- 1 tsp. garlic
- 1 tsp. salt
- 4 tbsp. lime juice
- 3 tbsp. cilantro, chopped

Serve with fresh vegetables or crackers. Also great as a sandwich spread.
Serves 12

In a sauté pan, combine the pepper, wine, and garlic. Simmer for 2 minutes. Place in a food processor with sour cream, mayonnaise, lime, cilantro, and salt. Blend until thoroughly combined.

Calories (kcal)	*38*
Total Fat (gm)	*0*
% Calories from Fat	*1%*
Cholesterol (mg)	*3*
Sodium (mg)	*289*

Appetizers and Hors d'Oeuvres

Sun-Dried Tomato-Stuffed Mushrooms

6 large mushroom caps
½ cup onion, chopped
1 tsp. olive oil
2 tbsp. garlic, minced
½ cup sun-dried tomatoes, chopped
1 cup white wine
1 tbsp. chives
1 cup bread crumbs
½ cup feta cheese, crumbled
2 tbsp. fresh basil, chopped

The stuffed mushrooms can be made a day in advance and baked just before serving.
Serves 6

Remove the stems from the mushrooms and reserve. Heat olive oil in a medium sauté pan. Sauté the onion and garlic. Add the chopped sun-dried tomatoes and mushroom stems. Combine thoroughly. Deglaze with white wine and chives, and cook 2 minutes. Remove from heat and combine with the bread crumbs, feta cheese, and basil, and stuff the mushrooms with filling. Bake in a 350-degree oven for 20 minutes.

Calories (kcal)	*158*
Total Fat (gm)	*4*
% Calories from Fat	*28%*
Cholesterol (mg)	*8*
Sodium (mg)	*378*

THE PENNINGTON COOKBOOK

Warm Spinach and Artichoke Dip

Vegetable cooking spray
2 tbsp. onion, chopped
1 tbsp. garlic, chopped
½ cup dry sherry
3 cups fresh spinach, chopped
8 ounces Neufchatel cheese
3 tbsp. Parmesan cheese, grated
½ cup artichoke hearts, drained, rinsed, chopped
1 lemon
½ cup basil, coarsely chopped
6 pita bread rounds, quartered and sliced

Serve this warm or at room temperature. This is also a great side dish in place of creamed spinach.
Serves 12

Heat a sauce pan with vegetable cooking spray. Add the onion and garlic and cook 1 minute. Add the cleaned, chopped spinach to the pan and gently wilt. Add the sherry and cook further 1 minute. Neufchatel cheese is the reduced-fat cream cheese found in your supermarket. Whip the cream cheese and Parmesan with a mixer. Add the cooked spinach mixture, artichoke hearts, lemon, and basil. Season with salt and pepper, if you wish. Serve with toasted, quartered pita bread.

Calories (kcal)	165
Total Fat (gm)	5
% Calories from Fat	30%
Cholesterol (mg)	15
Sodium (mg)	283

Wild Mushroom Torte

- 10 filo pastry sheets
- Olive oil cooking spray
- 8 pints assorted mushrooms, chopped
- ¼ cup shallot, minced
- ½ tbsp. garlic, minced
- ½ cup fat-free cream cheese
- 2 tbsp. fresh basil, chopped
- 1 tbsp. coarsely ground pepper
- Salt, to taste
- 1 package rye melba toast

I know that 8 pints of mushrooms sounds crazy, but you will love this wonderful pâté torte. Serve with a side of chutney as garnish. Serves 12

Defrost filo dough. Chop mushrooms in a food processor. In a large sauté pan, sauté mushrooms, shallots, and garlic. Cook until all the juices have cooked, released, and evaporated. (This is called a duxelle.) Allow to cool completely. Combine with the cream cheese, salt, basil, and pepper blend. In a small 6-inch spring form pan, lay a filo sheet down and fold into the edges of the pan. Lightly spray with olive oil. Lay another filo sheet over the first and repeat for 5 layers. Spoon the mushroom mixture inside. "Fluff" the filo around the sides of the pan and decorate with more filo sheets. Bake for 25 minutes at 375 degrees. Serve with toast.

Calories (kcal)	99
Total Fat (gm)	1
% Calories from Fat	12%
Cholesterol (mg)	3
Sodium (mg)	204

CHAPTER 2

Breakfast and Brunch

Apple-Spiced French Toast
Banana Nut Pancakes
Broiled Grapefruit with Vanilla Ginger Sugar
Cafe Brulot
Eggs Sardou
Fruit Bagel Pizza
Garlic Cheese Grits
Grillades and Garlic Cheese Grits
Pennington Granola
Salmon Hash with Horseradish-Dill Cream
Sweet Potato Pancakes
Vegetable Frittata

THE PENNINGTON COOKBOOK

Apple-Spiced French Toast

12 slices Texas cut bread, or hamburger buns
Vegetable cooking spray
1 quart skim milk
4 eggs
2 egg whites
¾ cup sugar
½ tsp. cinnamon
¼ tsp. nutmeg
3 Granny Smith apples
3 tbsp. powdered sugar

Rather than frying our French toast, we have baked the toast with delicious moist apples. If hosting a brunch for friends, feel free to let pan-soak in refrigerator overnight and just pop in the oven in the morning. Nothing could be simpler.
Serves 6

Spray a sheet pan with vegetable cooking spray. Line with baking paper, if available. Place bread in an even layer on sheet pan. In a separate bowl, whip the milk, eggs, egg whites, sugar, cinnamon, and nutmeg. Pour over the French toast and let sit for 30 minutes in refrigerator. Meanwhile, cut apples into thin slices. Preheat oven to 400 degrees. Layer apples on top of toast. Spray with vegetable cooking spray, and bake for 20 minutes. Slice and serve with powdered sugar.

Calories (kcal)	382
Total Fat (gm)	5
% Calories from Fat	12%
Cholesterol (mg)	124
Sodium (mg)	409

Banana Nut Pancakes

2 cups flour
1 tsp. salt
½ tsp. baking powder
¼ cup sugar
2 eggs
¼ cup skim milk
2 tbsp. canola oil
2 cups bananas, chopped
½ cup brown sugar

Pancakes are a perfect example of a quick bread that is naturally low in fat. Rather than adding bananas to the batter, here a delightful "syrup" much like Bananas Foster is served over the pancakes.
Serves 6

Combine the flour, salt, and baking powder in a mixing bowl. In a separate bowl, combine the sugar, milk, and oil. Whip until fully combined, then fold the wet ingredients with the dry ingredients. Heat a griddle with vegetable cooking spray.

½ cup raisins
½ cup water
½ cup Grapenuts cereal

Pour ½ cup pancake mix onto griddle. Cook until outer edges are brown and bubbles rise through the center. Flip and finish cooking on the other side. In a small sauce pan, combine the brown sugar and water, and melt over medium heat. Add the chopped bananas and raisins. Cook 1 minute, then add Grapenuts. Remove banana syrup from stove and pour over pancakes.

Calories (kcal)	384
Total Fat (gm)	7
% Calories from Fat	15%
Cholesterol (mg)	60
Sodium (mg)	441

Broiled Grapefruit with Vanilla Ginger Sugar

¾ cup sugar
3 tbsp. crystallized ginger, chopped
¾ tsp. vanilla
6 large pink grapefruit

You are sure to enjoy this beautiful dish, which was inspired by crème brûlée.
Serves 6

Preheat broiler. In an electric coffee/spice grinder, combine sugar, ginger, and vanilla and grind fine. Halve each grapefruit crosswise and run a knife around each section to loosen it from the membranes. Arrange grapefruits, cut side up, in a flameproof baking dish or baking pan just large enough to hold them in one layer, and sprinkle with sugar mixture. Broil grapefruits about 1½ inches from heat until sugar melts and tops begin to brown, 10-15 minutes. Serve grapefruits at room temperature.

Calories (kcal)	200
Total Fat (gm)	0.3
% Calories from Fat	1%
Cholesterol (mg)	5
Sodium (mg)	0

Cafe Brulot

2 lemons
1 orange
⅓ cup brown sugar
2 cinnamon sticks
1½ tbsp. whole cloves
½ cup Grand Marnier
½ cup brandy
4 cups dark roast coffee

This is a traditional coffee drink in Louisiana, especially in New Orleans restaurants. The presentation is great for entertaining, and the drink is delicious for a Sunday jazz brunch.
Serves 8

Peel long strips of citrus peel without the white pith from the lemons and orange. Combine the citrus peels with brown sugar, cinnamon, cloves, and Grand Marnier in a small sauce pan and cook at a low simmer for 3 minutes. Remove from heat. Add the brandy. Ignite the brandy with a long match, preferably in front of an amazed crowd of guests. Pour hot brewed coffee into mugs. Gradually pour flaming flavored brandy into coffee.

Calories (kcal)	149
Total Fat (gm)	0.4
% Calories from Fat	4%
Cholesterol (mg)	0
Sodium (mg)	10

Eggs Sardou

6 artichokes
2 lemons
1 tsp. salt
1 tbsp. garlic, minced
2 quarts fresh spinach, picked and stemmed
6 eggs
6 slices tomato
3 English muffins, split
¾ cup Saffron Aoili, recipe included

The flavors of spinach and artichoke have always been a great combination. Here they are used to accent a great egg dish.
Serves 6

Place artichokes, lemon, and salt in a steamer, and cook until tender, about 20 minutes. Remove the leaves, stem, and choke, leaving the round, saucer-shaped heart. Scrape and chop 1 cup of meat from the tips of the leaves. Drain the water from the pan, add the spinach and garlic, and cook until wilted. Fold the 1 cup of artichoke meat with spinach. Preheat an oven to 350 degrees. Toast English muffins. Place

Calories (kcal)	254
Total Fat (gm)	6
% Calories from Fat	18%
Cholesterol (mg)	181
Sodium (mg)	510

tomato slices on a sheet pan and bake for 3 minutes. Poach eggs in an egg poacher, or follow the next instructions.

Heat a sauce pan filled with 3 inches of water until water reaches a slow simmer. Add 2 tsp. of vinegar and 1 tsp. salt. Carefully crack an egg into the water and let the eggs poach for 4 minutes. To serve this elegant breakfast, place 1 baked tomato slice on each toasted muffin. Place the artichoke sauce on top of tomato, with ½ cup of spinach artichoke mixture in the saucer. Top with the poached egg and drizzle with aoili.

Fruit Bagel Pizza

3 bagels
¾ cup non-fat cream cheese
1 tbsp. honey
2 tbsp. applesauce
Pinch nutmeg
½ cup strawberries, cut
¼ cup blueberries
¼ cup peaches, cut
1 tbsp. honey

These little bagel pizzas are beautiful for a brunch buffet, but also great for midweek breakfasts on the run.
Serves 6

Preheat oven to 350 degrees. Split bagels and toast for 5 minutes. In a mixing bowl, mix the cheese, honey, apple sauce, and nutmeg. Spread on toasted bagels. Arrange fruit on top and drizzle with additional honey.

Calories (kcal)	167
Total Fat (gm)	1
% Calories from Fat	4%
Cholesterol (mg)	5
Sodium (mg)	370

Garlic Cheese Grits

1 cup grits, yellow
3¾ cups water
¼ tsp. salt
1 tsp. cracked black pepper
2 tbsp. garlic, minced
¾ cup sharp cheddar cheese, grated

These are fabulous with grillades, but can also be served as a side dish for any meat, poultry, or seafood for breakfast or dinner.
Serves 6

Combine the grits, garlic, water, and salt in a medium sauce pan. Bring to a boil, stirring constantly to prevent clumps. Cook for 10 minutes. Fold in the pepper blend and cheese. Place in a baking pan uncovered and bake for 25 minutes. Allow to rest 15 minutes before serving.

Calories (kcal)	158
Total Fat (gm)	5
% Calories from Fat	29%
Cholesterol (mg)	15
Sodium (mg)	182

Grillades and Garlic Cheese Grits

¾ lb. flank steak, lean and boneless
¾ tsp. garlic powder
¾ tsp. poultry seasoning
1 tbsp. cracked black pepper
1 tsp. kosher salt
4 tbsp. all-purpose flour, browned
Vegetable cooking spray
1 cup onion, chopped
½ cup green bell pepper, chopped

Grillades and grits is a Louisiana brunch tradition. If you have not tried them, you are in for a treat.
Serves 6

Combine the pepper blend, salt, flour, and garlic powder. Cut the steak into cubes and pound ½-inch to tenderize. Rub seasonings into steak meat. Heat a large roasting pan or Dutch oven with vegetable cooking spray. Brown the meat on all sides. Remove from pan and hold. Add the onions and bell pepper to the pan and sauté 2 minutes. Add the meat back. Then, while stirring, add the beef broth, crushed tomatoes, and bay leaf. Cook for 40 minutes, or until sauce has thickened to a rich consistency and meat is tender. Serve over garlic cheese grits or plain boiled grits.

Breakfast and Brunch

1 can low-sodium beef broth
1 can crushed tomatoes
2 each bay leaves
2 cups garlic cheese grits, recipe included

Calories (kcal)	333
Total Fat (gm)	7
% Calories from Fat	18%
Cholesterol (mg)	29
Sodium (mg)	560

Pennington Granola

1 quart Rice Krispies®
1 quart corn flakes
1½ quarts oats, rolled (raw)
3 egg whites
1 cup light brown sugar
1 tbsp. almond extract
1 cup sliced almonds, toasted
1 cup dried fruit, chopped

Pick whatever dried fruits you wish. My favorite blend is mixed plain dried apples and dried cranberries. Serve with chilled milk or yogurt. Also a great snack. Store in an airtight container for up to two weeks.
Serves 12

Using your hands, fold together in a large bowl the Rice Krispies, corn flakes, oats, brown sugar, egg whites, and almond extract. Consistency should be barely wet. Lay on sheet pans lined with baking paper no more that an inch in depth. Bake for 15 minutes. Remove from oven, and allow to cool. Pour into a mixing bowl. Add the dried fruit and toasted almonds.

Calories (kcal)	370
Total Fat (gm)	9
% Calories from Fat	22%
Cholesterol (mg)	0
Sodium (mg)	232

Salmon Hash with Horseradish-Dill Cream

1 lb. salmon fillet, 1 inch thick
1 lb. new potatoes, coarse chopped
Vegetable cooking spray
½ cup fennel bulbs, cored and chopped
½ cup onion, chopped
1 tsp. garlic, chopped
½ cup green onion, chopped
6 tbsp. low-fat sour cream, chilled
4 tbsp. horseradish, grated
3 tbsp. dill weed, fresh, chopped
6 eggs, poached

To poach eggs in the classic fashion, fill a sauce pan or rondo with 2 inches of water. Add enough apple cider vinegar to the water to just barely taste, about 1-2 tablespoons. Bring to a boil, then reduce heat to a simmer. Tiny bubbles should be slowly rolling at the edges of the pan. Crack eggs into water and allow to poach for 3-5 minutes, depending on the number and size of eggs. Remove with a slotted spoon onto paper towels and then onto plate.
Serves 6

Preheat an oven to 400 degrees. Place salmon fillets on baking sheet and cook for 12 minutes. Remove from oven and allow to cool. Meanwhile, steam chopped potatoes until just tender. Whip the sour cream, horseradish, and dill in a bowl and chill. Heat a large sauté pan with vegetable cooking spray. Sauté the fennel, onion, and garlic. Add the potatoes and green onion. Sauté until all ingredients are cooked through. Flake the salmon into the potato hash and fold until warmed through. Poach eggs in an egg poacher or in 3 inches of simmering water with a tsp. of vinegar added. Serve hash with an egg on top and horseradish sauce on the side.

Calories (kcal)	213
Total Fat (gm)	7
% Calories from Fat	31%
Cholesterol (mg)	221
Sodium (mg)	176

Sweet Potato Pancakes

3 russet potatoes, peeled and grated
3 sweet potatoes, peeled and grated

A great side dish for breakfast, lunch, or dinner. For great hash browns, cook potatoes loose rather than forming into pancakes.
Serves 6

Peel and grate the potato and sweet potatoes, and place in

3 egg whites
½ cup onion, grated
1 tsp. garlic powder
2 tbsp. chives, chopped
½ cup flour
Salt and pepper, to taste
Vegetable cooking spray

cold water to keep from discoloring. Heat a griddle or sauté pan with vegetable cooking spray. Squeeze out all the water possible from potatoes. Blend with egg whites, grated onion, garlic powder, chives, and flour, and season with salt and pepper. Form 3 tbsp. into small pancakes, and cook on the griddle until crispy and cooked through, about 3 minutes on each side.

Calories (kcal)	*133*
Total Fat (gm)	*0*
% Calories from Fat	*2%*
Cholesterol (mg)	*0*
Sodium (mg)	*86*

Vegetable Frittata

¼ cup sun-dried tomatoes, chopped
Vegetable cooking spray
1 cup onion, coarse chopped
½ cup carrot, coarse chopped
½ cup celery, coarse chopped
½ cup green bell pepper, coarse chopped
1 cup new potatoes, quartered, blanched
3 cups Egg Beaters® 99% egg substitute
5 eggs, whipped
2 tbsp. parsley, chopped
Salt and pepper, to taste

A cast-iron skillet works wonderfully for this frittata because it holds the heat so well. If you do not have one, sauté in a pan and transfer to a baking dish.
Serves 6

Preheat oven to 350 degrees. Soak sun-dried tomatoes in ½ cup warm water. Heat a 10-inch cast-iron skillet with vegetable cooking spray. Sauté the onion until caramelized. Add the carrot and cook until tender. Add celery and green bell pepper. Cook until tender before adding the potatoes and sun-dried tomatoes. Remove from pan, and mix with eggs, egg substitute, and parsley. Return to pan, and bake in a 350-degree oven for 20 minutes.

Calories (kcal)	*135*
Total Fat (gm)	*4*
% Calories from Fat	*25%*
Cholesterol (mg)	*151*
Sodium (mg)	*380*

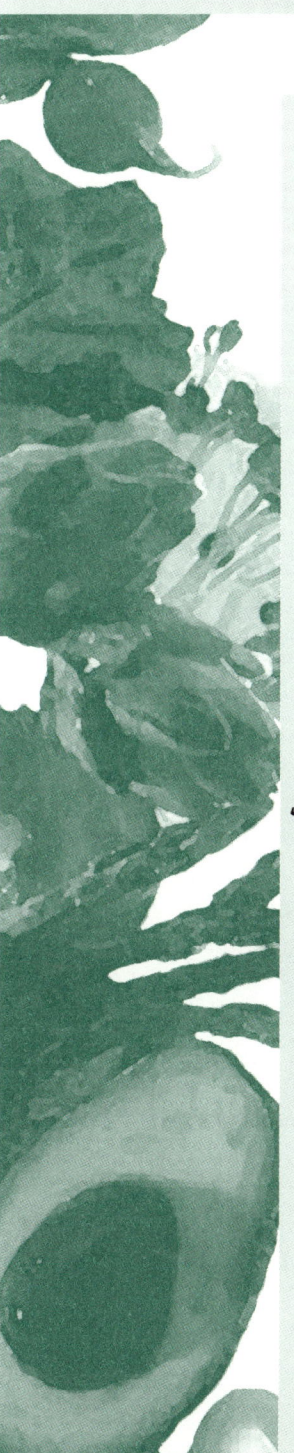

CHAPTER 3

Salads and Sandwiches

Arugula with an Orange Vinaigrette
Baby Greens Salad with Spring Herb Dressing
Chilled Pickled Slaw
Chinese Chop Salad
Creamy Dill and Horseradish Potato Salad
Early Spring Blue Crab Salad
Grilled Shrimp and Curried Lentil Salad
Hoisin Hoagie
Italian Muffaletta Sandwich
Japanese Noodle Salad
Mardi Gras Salad
Niçoise Pasta Salad
Open-Faced Corned Beef Sandwich
Remoulade Seafood Dumpling Salad
Roasted Garlic, Brie, and Apple Sandwich
Roasted Onion and Garlic Salad
Saged Roast Duck Salad with Pear Vinaigrette
Smoked Salmon and Watercress Sandwich
Southern Vegetable Poboy
Spinach and Basil Salad with Cajun Tasso Vinaigrette
Summer Tomato Salad

Arugula with an Orange Vinaigrette

⅓ cup orange juice
¼ cup extra virgin olive oil
2 tbsp. balsamic vinegar
3 lb. fennel bulbs, thinly sliced
3 bunches arugula
5 oranges, peeled and cubed
4 oz. Parmesan cheese

Sometimes the simplest salads are the best salads. Here is an example. Be sure to remove any pith from the oranges and any greens from the core of the fennel. This will only add bitter flavor, which is fine for such a sweet dressing, but the arugula will be the perfect balance.
Serves 8

Combine the orange juice, oil, and vinegar in a small bowl or cup. Cut the skins from the oranges and dice. Do not just peel oranges or they may be bitter. Toss arugula, fennel, oranges, cheese, and dressing.

Calories (kcal)	202
Total Fat (gm)	11
% Calories from Fat	48%
Cholesterol (mg)	11
Sodium (mg)	332

Baby Greens Salad with Spring Herb Dressing

1 tbsp. basil
1 tbsp. chives
1 tbsp. thyme
½ tbsp. oregano or marjoram
1 tbsp. dill
1 tbsp. sage
1 cup Italian parsley
2 tbsp. lemon zest
4 tbsp. extra virgin olive oil
3 tbsp. lemon juice

The secret to this recipe lies in the technique of macerating or crushing the herbs in the oil to gradually release herbaceous flavor. Handpicking lettuce leaves does not require you to go out in a vegetable patch with garden gloves. Grocery stores offer wonderful salad greens either separately or as a mix found in a bag. Please handpick so that you balance mild flavors with colorful but slightly bitter flavors, such as red radicchio or the chartreuse frisse and endive.
Serves 12

Individually coarse-chop all the herbs and combine in a bowl. Add the olive oil and crush with the back of a spoon. Allow to sit at room temperature for 20 minutes, "mashing" once in a

Salads and Sandwiches

- 6 cups baby lettuce leaves, handpicked
- 1 loaf French bread, sliced
- Pinch salt, pepper and sugar, to taste

while. Meanwhile, toast the sliced bread and clean and pick the lettuce leaves. Add the lemon juice to dressing and season with salt, pepper, and sugar. Toss salad and serve with a toasted bread crouton.

Calories (kcal)	165
Total Fat (gm)	6
% Calories from Fat	32%
Cholesterol (mg)	0
Sodium (mg)	240

Chilled Pickled Slaw

- 1 large cabbage, shaved
- 1 yellow onion, thinly sliced
- 1 green bell pepper, diced
- 3/4 cup sugar
- 1 tbsp. turmeric, ground
- 3 tbsp. canola oil
- 1 cup apple cider vinegar
- 1 tsp. celery seed
- 1 tsp. dried mustard
- 1/2 tbsp. salt

This is a wonderful side salad dish great for picnics, but also fabulous served on sandwiches with your favorite lean meats and fresh buns. The slaw will hold in a refrigerator for up to 3 weeks.

Serves 12

Shave the cabbage 1/4-inch thick, and toss with onion and bell pepper. In a small sauce pan, combine the sugar, turmeric, vinegar, celery seed, dry mustard, and salt. Bring to a simmer, then remove from heat, stirring until sugar is dissolved. Add the oil to vinegar mixture. Pour the hot liquid over cabbage, allow to cool, and marinate for at least 12 hours before serving.

Calories (kcal)	103
Total Fat (gm)	4
% Calories from Fat	30%
Cholesterol (mg)	0
Sodium (mg)	279

Chinese Chop Salad

3 boned and skinned chicken breast halves
Vegetable cooking spray
2 cups Napa cabbage, sliced
¼ cup cilantro, picked
½ cup water chestnuts, sliced
1 cup mushrooms, sliced
½ cup red bell pepper, seeded and diced
2 tbsp. jalapeno pepper, seeded and minced
¼ cup tomatoes, seeded and chopped
1 cup bean sprouts
½ cup carrot, grated
1 tbsp. ginger root, minced
1 tbsp. garlic, minced
¼ cup soy sauce
¼ cup rice wine vinegar
1 tbsp. sesame oil
1 tbsp. sesame seeds

Napa cabbage is the football-shaped head of cabbage with delicate crinkled leaves found in the Oriental fresh vagetable section of many grocery stores. Rather than tossing this salad, actively chop it on a cutting board until all the flavors have married. Don't forget the chopsticks!
Serves 6

Roast the chicken breasts in a preheated 350-degree oven for 15 minutes. Combine the soy sauce, rice wine vinegar, garlic, ginger root, and chicken stock. Deglaze the pan with sauce to add extra flavor. To do this, when chicken is done, remove chicken from the roasting pan and add the sauce to the pan, stirring until all of the caramelized juices have released from the bottom of the pan. Place back into a bowl, and add the sesame oil. Combine all of the remaining ingredients. Place tossed ingredients on a cutting board. Chop all of the ingredients together until the chicken is in bite-size pieces and all ingredients are well blended.

Calories (kcal)	125
Total Fat (gm)	4
% Calories from Fat	29%
Cholesterol (mg)	26
Sodium (mg)	599

Creamy Dill and Horseradish Potato Salad

- 3 lb. red potatoes, cooked and drained
- 1 cup celery, chopped
- ½ cup green onion, chopped
- 1¼ cups fat-free mayonnaise
- ½ cup fat-free sour cream
- ⅓ cup fresh dill, chopped
- ¼ cup Parmesan cheese, grated
- 3 tbsp. lemon juice
- 1½ tbsp. garlic, minced
- 1 tbsp. Worcestershire sauce
- 1 tsp. cracked black pepper
- 3 tbsp. horseradish, prepared

Serve as a cold side salad or warm with meats and seafood. Great recipe to bring along for a tailgate party served with barbecued chicken or roast beef sandwiches.
Serves 12

Cut potatoes into quarters. Steam or boil potatoes in water until tender. Chill in a refrigerator. In a mixing bowl, combine the mayonnaise, sour cream, dill, cheese, lemon, garlic, horseradish, and Worcestershire sauce. Mix until well combined. Fold in the potatoes, celery, and green onion and mix for 15 seconds to combine and lightly cream. Place back in the cooler to chill, but adjust seasoning before you serve.

Calories (kcal)	113
Total Fat (gm)	1
% Calories from Fat	6%
Cholesterol (mg)	3
Sodium (mg)	288

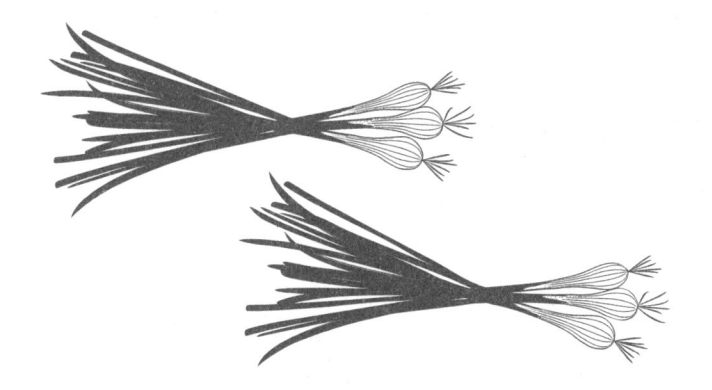

Early Spring Blue Crab Salad

3 red potatoes, wedges
Salt and pepper, to taste
1 tbsp. olive oil
¾ cup corn flour, or masa
Pinch cayenne pepper
6 soft shell crabs, split in half
2 cups crab meat
½ cup red onion, sliced thin
1½ cups cucumber, sliced
1 cup leeks, sliced thin
1 cup fennel, sliced thin
2 tsp. champagne wine vinegar
1 tsp. sage, chopped

This is definitely an entree salad fit for a king . . . or your closest friends! Serve with a fresh loaf of bread to savor anything left on the plate.
Serves 6

Preheat an oven to 350 degrees. Season the potatoes with salt and pepper, and one tsp. olive oil in a stainless bowl. Reserve the bowl. Lay potatoes on a sheet pan and roast in the oven for 30 minutes. Toss the cornmeal and cayenne in a separate bowl. Coat the soft shell crabs in cornmeal. Heat a cast-iron skillet with remaining olive oil, sauté the crabs on each side. Remove crabs from the pan, and remove pan from the heat. Add the crab meat to warm pan and lightly toss in pan to barely heat. In the reserved seasoned bowl, toss the fennel, leeks, red onion, cucumber, champagne vinegar, and sage. Serve the soft shell crab on the vegetable salad, dressed with crabmeat and roasted potatoes.

Calories (kcal)	*499*
Total Fat (gm)	*21*
% Calories from Fat	*39%*
Cholesterol (mg)	*85*
Sodium (mg)	*1278*

Grilled Shrimp and Curried Lentil Salad

2 lb. medium shrimp, peeled and veined
Bamboo skewers, soaked in water
1 tsp. black pepper
½ cup onion, chopped
2 tsp. garlic, chopped

To bring out more full flavor in spices, such as the curry in this dish, it is good to toast them in a shallow pan under low heat. Once the brilliant aroma rises, or blooms, the spices are ready. Enjoy this salad with flat bread and jasmine tea for a picnic lunch outside.
Serves 6

Toss the peeled and veined shrimp with pepper. Skewer on bamboo skewers and grill or broil until just cooked but juicy,

2 tbsp. curry powder, toasted
½ tbsp. paprika
1 cup lentils
1 tsp. kosher salt
¾ cup carrots, diced
½ cup green onion, sliced
1 lemon
½ cup plain yogurt

about 5 minutes. Transfer to a bowl. In a medium sauce pan, combine the onion, garlic, curry powder, paprika, and lentils. Cover with water up to 1 inch over lentils. Bring to a simmer, reduce heat and cook 15 minutes. Lentils should be tender but firm to the tooth for a salad. Add the lentils to the bowl. Add the carrot and green onion. Toss with lemon juice and yogurt. Serve chilled or at room temperature.

Calories (kcal)	197
Total Fat (gm)	4
% Calories from Fat	17%
Cholesterol (mg)	232
Sodium (mg)	603

Hoisin Hoagie

½ loaf French bread
1 lb. pork tenderloin
2 tbsp. hoisin sauce
1 tbsp. soy sauce
1 cup cilantro, picked
2 cups Napa cabbage, shredded
½ cup red bell pepper, julienne
½ cup carrot, grated
1 tsp. hoisin sauce
1 tsp. soy sauce
2 tsp. sesame oil
1 tsp. jalapeno, minced

East meets West in this delicious sandwich. The soy sauce and hoisin sauce will be very high in sodium, so moderate portion sizes if you are lowering the sodium in your diet. Serve with baked won ton chips and oranges for an Asian flair.
Serves 6

Roll the pork tenderloin in 2 tbsp. hoisin sauce and 1 tbsp. soy sauce. Roast in a 400-degree oven for 20 minutes. Meanwhile, slice the French bread into 4 portions and cut for sandwiches. In a bowl, toss the cabbage, cilantro, bell pepper, carrot, the remaining hoisin sauce and soy sauce, sesame oil, and jalapeno together. Slice the pork loin super thin across the grain. Divide among the sandwiches and top with cabbage mixture.

Calories (kcal)	251
Total Fat (gm)	6
% Calories from Fat	23%
Cholesterol (mg)	50
Sodium (mg)	472

Italian Muffaletta Sandwich

1 loaf Italian bread
18 oz. turkey pastrami, sliced thin
6 oz. feta cheese, crumbled
½ cup carrot, chopped
¼ cup celery, chopped
¼ cup red onion, chopped
¼ cup capers, rinsed
2 anchovies, minced
4 Greek olives, chopped
¼ cup scallions, chopped
1 tsp. fennel seed
½ tbsp. coarsely ground pepper
1 tbsp. champagne wine vinegar
6 Roma tomatoes, sliced

A muffaletta sandwich is a large sandwich that layers Italian cold cuts and olive salad on a special loaf of Italian bread, called muffaletta—thus its name. Here we have trimmed the sandwich in calories and fat and kept the fabulous textures and flavors.
Serves 6

In a bowl, combine the carrot, celery, onion, olives, capers, anchovy, fennel, pepper, champagne wine vinegar, and scallions. If champagne wine vinegar is not available, substitute a high quality white wine vinegar. Let marinate overnight. To make sandwiches, layer turkey pastrami, feta, tomatoes, and olive salad.

Calories (kcal)	445
Total Fat (gm)	15
% Calories from Fat	31%
Cholesterol (mg)	72
Sodium (mg)	1772

Japanese Noodle Salad

3 tbsp. sesame seeds, toasted
1 lb. soba noodles (or buckwheat noodles)
3 tbsp. peanut oil
1 tbsp. sesame oil
½ cup rice wine vinegar
1½ cups cucumber, julienned

Soba noodles are also called buckwheat noodles. They can be found in most large grocery stores, but if not available there, look for them in an Asian market or health food store. The delicious nutty flavor is worth looking for.
Serves 8

Bring a large pot of salted water to a rolling boil. Cook soba noodles until tender. Drain and plunge into an iced water bath. Drain once more. Toss noodles with peanut oil and

1 cup carrot, julienned
½ cup radishes, thinly sliced
½ cup green onion, thinly sliced
Salt and pepper, to taste
¼ cup peanuts, crushed

sesame oil and toss well to coat. Fold noodles with vinegar, cucumber, carrot, radishes, and green onion. Season with salt and pepper to taste. Garnish with peanuts.

Calories (kcal)	*315*
Total Fat (gm)	*11*
% Calories from Fat	*30%*
Cholesterol (mg)	*0*
Sodium (mg)	*463*

Mardi Gras Salad

4 oranges
¼ cup cane vinegar, or wine vinegar
2 tbsp. walnut oil
¼ tsp. cumin, ground
3 tbsp. shallots, minced
1 tbsp. garlic, chopped
3 cups spinach, cleaned and veined
3 cups Boston lettuce, torn
2 cups red cabbage, shaved
¼ cup sunflower seeds
Salt and pepper, to taste

This salad is so named for the brilliant colors of carnival—purple, gold, and green. It is festive for anytime of year, however.
Serves 6

Remove skins from oranges and membranes, leaving orange sections. Reserve any orange juices, and squeeze any juices from membranes. Combine the orange juice, vinegar, walnut oil, cumin, shallots, and garlic. Season with salt and pepper. Toss the spinach and Boston lettuce in dressing, and garnish with cabbage, oranges, and sunflower seeds.

Calories (kcal)	*113*
Total Fat (gm)	*7*
% Calories from Fat	*41%*
Cholesterol (mg)	*0*
Sodium (mg)	*22*

Niçoise Pasta Salad

8 oz. pasta shells
¾ lb. tuna steaks
Vegetable cooking spray
1 tsp. coarsely ground pepper
¼ cup white wine
¼ cup chicken stock, or low-sodium broth
3 tsp. garlic, chopped
¼ cup red onion, chopped
¼ cup celery, seeded and chopped
¼ cup Roma tomatoes, seeded and chopped
¼ cup artichoke hearts, quartered
¾ cup green beans, blanched
2 tbsp. basil, chopped
2 tbsp. Italian parsley, chopped
¼ cup green onion, chopped
¼ cup Parmesan cheese, grated
¼ cup Niçoise olives, pitted
Salt and pepper, to taste
¾ cup sourdough bread, sliced
1 tbsp. extra virgin olive oil

The flavors of the Mediterranean come from fresh produce and seafood to make this salad very special. Serve hot for a warm pasta, or cold as a salad.
Serves 6

Put 1 gallon of salted water on the stove to come to a boil. Once the water is rapidly boiling, add the pasta and cook until it is soft in the center but still has a bite to the tooth. Drain in a colander. Heat a large sauté pan sprayed with vegetable cooking spray. Season the tuna steaks with pepper, and sear steaks in pan 2 minutes on each side. Remove from pan. With the grain, tear the steaks into bite-size chunks.

While the pan is still warm, add the white wine and chicken broth. Reduce to ¾ cup of rich aromatic dressing. In a large bowl, fold the pasta, tuna, garlic, red onion, celery, tomato, artichoke, green beans, basil, parsley, and green onion. Add dressing to moisten. Toss lightly and adjust seasoning with salt and pepper. Brush bread slices with olive oil and toast. Serve salad warm or at room temperature with a light sprinkle of Parmesan, garnish of olives, and toasts.

Calories (kcal)	394
Total Fat (gm)	10
% Calories from Fat	23%
Cholesterol (mg)	24
Sodium (mg)	464

Open-Faced Corned Beef Sandwich

2 lb. corned beef brisket, thinly sliced
¾ cup plain low-fat yogurt
½ cup non-fat sour cream
½ cup prepared horseradish
1½ tbsp. lemon juice
8 slices rye bread, toasted
1 quart arugula, washed
16 slices tomato
8 slices red onion
Cracked black pepper, to taste

Arugula is a wonderful flavor to pair with the salty rich flavor of corned beef. Either purchase your corned beef already prepared or make one fresh.
Serves 8

Heat a clean griddle on medium. Griddle the corned beef until warm. In a small bowl, combine the yogurt, sour cream, horseradish, and lemon. To assemble, top the toasted rye bread with a little dressing, add arugula and tomato, and top with warm corned beef. Finish with a little more dressing, onion, and cracked black pepper.

Calories (kcal)	*450*
Total Fat (gm)	*19*
% Calories from Fat	*38%*
Cholesterol (mg)	*64*
Sodium (mg)	*418*

Remoulade Seafood Dumpling Salad

Remoulade is a sweet and salty dressing just perfect for seafood dishes. This salad is delightful for any occasion.
Serves 6

Dumplings:
12 won ton wrappers
½ cup crawfish, minced
¼ cup crab meat
¼ cup shrimp, cooked, minced
3 tbsp. bell pepper, minced
1 tbsp. red onion, minced
1 tsp. garlic, minced
2 egg whites
2 cups chicken stock

Dressing:
1 cup fat-free mayonnaise
¼ cup pickle relish
3 tbsp. red onion, minced
3 tbsp. capers, chopped
2 tbsp. tarragon, chopped
3 tbsp. lemon juice
1 tsp. tomato paste
Pinch cayenne pepper

Salad:
6 sprigs Italian parsley
4 cups baby lettuce leaves
12 shrimp, cooked
1 cup crawfish, cooked
1 cup crab meat
1 lemon

In a bowl, fold the chopped crawfish, shrimp, crab, peppers, garlic, red onion, and egg whites. Place 2 tsp. of stuffing in the middle of a won ton wrapper. Wet the edges of wrapper with water, fold 4 edges up to center, and seal edges together. Place in a steamer and steam with chicken stock for 10 minutes.

Meanwhile, mix the mayonnaise, relish, onion, capers, garlic, lemon juice, tomato paste, and cayenne. Toss the greens in lemon juice and place the baby greens on plates. Place steamed dumplings on plates, and garnish with cooked seafood. Serve with remoulade sauce and garnish with parsley.

Calories (kcal)	254
Total Fat (gm)	3
% Calories from Fat	11%
Cholesterol (mg)	140
Sodium (mg)	764

Roasted Garlic, Brie, and Apple Sandwich

- 2 heads garlic
- 1 loaf French bread, toasted
- ½ tsp. apple cider vinegar
- 4 oz. Brie
- 3 oz. fat-free cream cheese, sliced
- 4 tbsp. toasted almonds, chopped
- 3 tsp. Dijon mustard
- 3 Granny Smith apples, cored, skinned, sliced
- 2 cups Boston lettuce leaves, torn

Use strong-flavored cheeses, such as a ripe Brie, or substitute blue cheese, Gorgonzola, or a ripe Parmesan. You will find a little will go a long way, and you won't be deprived of great cheese flavor. Serve with a pasta salad on the side and fruit-flavored iced tea. For canapés at your next shower, serve with sliced white bread and cut the outer crusts from the bread.
Serves 6

Preheat an oven to 375 degrees. Cut garlic in half across the cloves. Place in a baking dish with 2 tbsp. of water, cover, and roast for 35-45 minutes. Meanwhile, slice the loaf of bread into 6 equal slices, then cut in half to prepare sandwiches.

Mix the Brie with fat-free cream cheese. Transfer to a clean working space lined with plastic wrap. Wrap cheese and mold into a log shape. Place in refrigerator for 5 minutes, then unwrap and roll in crushed walnuts.

When garlic is finished roasting, it will be soft. Squeeze it out of the garlic pods. Prepare your bread by spreading the roasted garlic on a slice of bread. Spread some mustard on bottom half. Cut slices of cheese from the chilled Brie cheese log. Top with apple slices and lettuce.

Calories (kcal)	*356*
Total Fat (gm)	*11*
% Calories from Fat	*27%*
Cholesterol (mg)	*21*
Sodium (mg)	*690*

Roasted Onion and Garlic Salad

2 small red onions
6 heads garlic, small
2 tbsp. fresh herbs (parsley, sage, thyme, etc., chopped
3 tbsp. balsamic vinegar
1 cup vegetable stock, or low-sodium broth
1 tbsp. balsamic vinegar
2 tbsp. extra virgin olive oil
2 heads red leaf lettuce, cleaned
1 loaf Italian bread

Serve as an entree salad or a side salad to accompany a rich, warm winter entrée.
Serves 6

Preheat an oven to 375 degrees. Cut red onions into wedges, leaving the core intact. Toss with 3 tbsp. balsamic vinegar, 1 tbsp. olive oil, and fresh herbs. Lay on a sheet pan and roast in the oven for 25-30 minutes. Cut whole heads of garlic in half with skins intact. Lay cut side facing up in a baking dish. Fill dish with ¼ inch of water. Cover with foil and roast in oven for 45 minutes or until soft, caramelized, and sweetly aromatic. Remove onions and deglaze the hot pan with vegetable broth. Combine deglazed broth in a small sauce pan. Add any remaining broth. Squeeze the garlic out of 2 roasted heads into broth. Whisk together and reduce to 1 cup.

Remove from heat and add 1 tbsp. balsamic vinegar and 1 tbsp. olive oil. Toss the roasted garlic dressing with lettuces and roasted onions. Serve each person salad with a half head of roasted garlic to spread on bread.

Calories (kcal)	276
Total Fat (gm)	7
% Calories from Fat	22%
Cholesterol (mg)	0
Sodium (mg)	533

Saged Roast Duck Salad with Pear Vinaigrette

Vegetable cooking spray
2 lb. duck breast, boned and skinned
½ tsp. kosher salt
Pinch white pepper
1 tbsp. sage, chopped fine

If you can find pear vinegar, substitute it for the apple cider vinegar. It will accentuate the refreshing flavor even more.
Serves 6

Heat a medium sauté pan with vegetable cooking spray. Trim duck breasts of any fat and skin. Season with salt, pepper, and sage. Sauté breasts for 8 minutes, or until cooked

Salads and Sandwiches

¼ cup apple cider vinegar
½ cup duck or chicken stock
2 cups ripe pears, cored and chopped
6 cups Boston lettuce, washed and torn
6 slices pumpernickel bread, toasted

through. Remove from the pan. Turn off the heat, then add the apple cider vinegar and stock. Cook for 2 minutes, then add the pears. Cook an additional 2 minutes, or until pears are tender. Toss the lettuce with the warm pear dressing. Slice the duck breasts and divide among the salads. Serve with toasted pumpernickel toasts.

Calories (kcal)	*323*
Total Fat (gm)	*11*
% Calories from Fat	*39%*
Cholesterol (mg)	*117*
Sodium (mg)	*551*

Smoked Salmon and Watercress Sandwich

6 onion and garlic bagels, sliced and toasted
1 cup fat-free cream cheese
2 tbsp. lemon juice
1 tbsp. carrot, grated
1 tbsp. celery, minced
1 tbsp. green onion, minced
4 cups watercress
¾ lb. smoked salmon
2 tomatoes, sliced

Have someone help you slice the smoked salmon paper thin. Smoked salmon, or gravelox, is a delicacy prized for its silky texture. When this sandwich is perfectly matched with crispy watercress, you'll just love it.
Serves 6

With a mixer, whip the cream cheese with lemon. Fold in carrot, celery, and green onion. Spread cheese on toasted bagels, layer with salmon, watercress, and tomato, and serve.

Calories (kcal)	*321*
Total Fat (gm)	*4*
% Calories from Fat	*11%*
Cholesterol (mg)	*20*
Sodium (mg)	*1078*

Southern Vegetable Poboy

2 loaves French bread, lightly toasted
Vegetable cooking spray
1 small eggplant, cut in strips
½ red onion, thinly sliced
1 red bell pepper, julienne
1 tbsp. extra virgin olive oil
1 tsp. cracked black pepper
2 Creole tomatoes, sliced thin
1 carrot, grated
2 cups spinach, sliced
½ cup fat-free mayonnaise
¼ cup Creole mustard
1 lemon

A poboy is a Louisiana submarine sandwich or hoagie. The French bread of Louisiana is very light, soft, and sweet in the center, with a thin, crisp crust on the outside. Other Italian or French loaves will be fine with this recipe, but one day you must try the Louisiana version. Creole mustard is coarse grained, and Creole tomatoes are large, red, and ripe.
Serves 6

Preheat an oven to 375 degrees. Slice the eggplant ½-inch thick into rounds, then into strips. Slice the onions and bell pepper thin. Toss the eggplant, bell pepper, and onion with olive oil and pepper, and lay on a sheet pan sprayed with vegetable cooking spray. Roast in oven for 15 minutes. Meanwhile, blend the mayonnaise and Creole mustard with the juice from the lemon. To prepare sandwiches, spread bread with Creole mustard dressing and stack the eggplant, onion, and bell pepper on bottom of sandwich. Finish with spinach and tomato before covering with bread.

Calories (kcal)	108
Total Fat (gm)	3
% Calories from Fat	26%
Cholesterol (mg)	0
Sodium (mg)	364

Spinach and Basil Salad with Cajun Tasso Vinaigrette

½ cup tasso ham, minced
½ cup onion, chopped
1 tbsp. garlic, minced
1 tbsp. canola oil
½ cup sugar
½ cup red wine vinegar
Salt and pepper, to taste

The texture and size of basil leaves allow this delicious herb to be used not only for flavor enhancement but also as a salad green.
Serves 6

For the warm vinaigrette, heat canola oil in a small sauce pan and saute the tasso, onion, and garlic. Add the sugar and vinegar and cook 2 minutes. Season with salt and pepper.

2 red onions, quartered
2 tbsp. balsamic vinegar
½ loaf sourdough bread
6 cups fresh spinach, cleaned, stemmed, torn
2 cups fresh basil leaves
3 hard-boiled eggs, peeled and quartered
2 large Creole tomatoes

Preheat an oven to 375 degrees. Toss the quartered onions in balsamic vinegar. Place on a sheet pan, cover, and roast for 30 minutes. Tear the bread into large, coarse pieces and toast in the oven. Lightly toss croutons in 2 tsp. vinaigrette. Toss spinach and basil in remaining vinaigrette. Serve spinach with roasted red onions, croutons, eggs, and tomatoes.

Calories (kcal)	*196*
Total Fat (gm)	*6*
% Calories from Fat	*38%*
Cholesterol (mg)	*25*
Sodium (mg)	*295*

Summer Tomato Salad

½ tbsp. extra virgin olive oil
1 tsp. champagne wine vinegar
Kosher salt, to taste
1 cup green leaf lettuce, cleaned and torn
1 cup arugula leaves, or spinach
1 bunch fresh basil
2 tomatoes, red ripe
1 pint cherry tomatoes, stemmed
½ red onion, thinly sliced
2 tbsp. Parmesan cheese, shaved
Cracked black pepper, to taste

The success of this recipe relies on the quality of its ingredients. This is a great lesson to be learned for any recipe, especially when cooking healthier for today's lifestyles. Tomatoes come in so many colors and flavors today. Experiment and enjoy the freshness of summer.
Serves 6

Lightly toss the lettuce, arugula, and basil leaves with olive oil, vinegar, and salt in a stainless bowl. Remove to chilled plates or platter. Add the tomatoes and red onion to bowl, and lightly toss to season in remaining flavors. Arrange on salad greens. Garnish with Parmesan and cracked black pepper.

Calories (kcal)	*53*
Total Fat (gm)	*2*
% Calories from Fat	*33%*
Cholesterol (mg)	*1*
Sodium (mg)	*51*

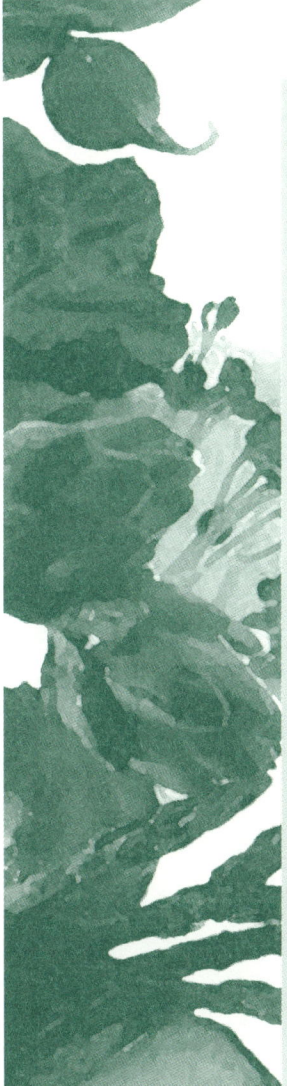

CHAPTER 4

Soups and Stews

Chili Verde
Corn and Shrimp Chowder with Saged Croutons
Crawfish Bisque with Crawfish Croutons
Fish Soup with Garlic and Escarole
Italian Bean and Pasta Soup
Mexican Hominy Stew
New England Clam Chowder
Potato and Leek Soup with Asiago Croutons
Pumpkin Velouté
Smoked Chicken and Okra Gumbo
Southwestern Chili
Spinach, Oyster, and Artichoke Soup
Vegetable Orecchiette Soup
El Xochitl (Chicken Soup Fiesta)

Chili Verde

- 2 tbsp. canola oil
- 2 lb. turkey breast, boneless and skinless, cut in ½-inch pieces
- ¼ cup cornmeal
- 1 tbsp. cumin, ground
- 1 quart green onion, chopped
- 1 quart low-sodium chicken broth
- 1 cup canned green chilies, chopped
- 1 cup cilantro, chopped
- 1 avocado, sliced
- 8 flour tortillas, warmed
- 2 cups tomato salsa

Chili Verde basically means green chili. Prepare this as spicy as you wish. If you are able to purchase Masa Harina, use it rather than the cornmeal to thicken your chili. It will add a nice smoky flavor.

Serves 8

Heat the canola oil in a large soup pot. Sauté the turkey pieces until opaque in color. Add the cumin and cornmeal, and cook a further 2 minutes, stirring to coat. Add green onions, chilies, and chicken broth. Cook for 10 minutes or until chili thickens. Serve with avocado slices, warmed tortillas, and salsa on the side.

Calories (kcal)	*352*
Total Fat (gm)	*13*
% Calories from Fat	*31%*
Cholesterol (mg)	*49*
Sodium (mg)	*542*

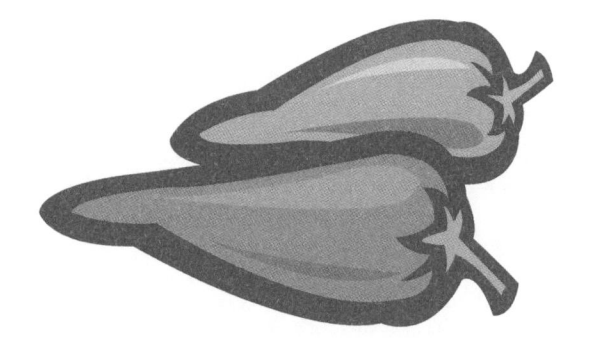

Corn and Shrimp Chowder with Saged Croutons

4 ears corn, husked
2 lb. shrimp, unpeeled, with heads
2 bay leaves
1 sprig thyme
1 sprig sage
Salt and pepper, to taste
1 tbsp. corn oil
½ cup onion, chopped
1 tbsp. garlic, minced
4 red potatoes, cubed
1 loaf sourdough bread
1 tbsp. corn oil
1 tsp. garlic powder
2 tsp. sage, minced

The secret to this chowder is in the stock. A lot of flavor is found in corn husks and cobs. Maximize the sweet corn flavor by using the cobs in the stock. Likewise, maximize flavor with the shrimp shells. Serve the chowder with hot biscuits and a green salad. This is wonderful for a middle of the week menu.
Serves 6

Cut the corn from the cobs, scraping cobs to collect "corn milk." Reserve. Peel and head the shrimp. In a large stock pot over medium heat, dry sauté the shells and heads to dry them out. The shells should be brittle. Add the corn cobs, bay, thyme, sage sprig, and season with salt and pepper. Cover with water and bring to a boil. Reduce heat to a simmer and cook at least 30 minutes, or until shrimp and corn flavor prevails.

Strain the stock in a fine mesh strainer, disregarding shells and cobs. In a soup pot, sauté the onion and garlic in corn oil. Add the corn kernels, milk, and potatoes. Add 2 quarts of crab and corn stock. Bring to a simmer and cook until potatoes are cooked through and tender. Add the shrimp and cook a further 5 minutes. Heat an oven to 350 degrees. Cut or tear the bread into pieces the size of large marbles. Toss bread with 1 tbsp. of corn oil, garlic powder, sage, and pinch of salt. Bake until crispy. Serve soup with croutons.

Calories (kcal)	*314*
Total Fat (gm)	*8*
% Calories from Fat	*23%*
Cholesterol (mg)	*230*
Sodium (mg)	*313*

Crawfish Bisque with Crawfish Croutons

2 lb. crawfish tails
½ cup flour
Vegetable cooking spray
1 cup onion, chopped
1 tbsp. garlic, chopped
½ cup green bell pepper, chopped
¼ cup red bell pepper, chopped
1 cup white wine
1 quart crawfish stock, or beef broth
½ cup bread crumbs
1 tbsp. fresh herbs
2 egg whites, whipped
2 cups cooked white rice

Calories (kcal)	390
Total Fat (gm)	6
% Calories from Fat	17%
Cholesterol (mg)	183
Sodium (mg)	429

Although shellfish such as crawfish are fairly high in dietary cholesterol, they also are fairly low in fat and calories. If you weigh the nutritional balances, shellfish are excellent once or twice a week for variety in planning menus. If you have never eaten crawfish, you have to try this crawfish dish first. This soup may be served as a beginning course to a meal. But with such rich, hearty flavor, it can also stand on its own as a main course. Serve a large bowl of bisque and crawfish croutons with a relish plate of pickled okra, green beans, and olives and a basket of hot corn bread.
Serves 6

Buy 8 pounds of crawfish, if they are available. Flash in boiling water, peel, and reserve the tails. Roast the shells in a 350-degree oven for 25 minutes. Prepare a stock with the roasted shells, some onion, garlic, tomato, and bay. Strain the stock and reserve. If whole crawfish are not available, make a stock from shrimp shells and use frozen crawfish tails. Coarse chop the crawfish tails.

   On medium heat, brown the flour in a soup kettle. Remove from pan. Spray kettle with cooking spray and saute the onion and garlic until brown and caramelized. Add the peppers and crawfish. Remove half the crawfish mixture from the pan and place in a bowl. Sprinkle the remaining crawfish mixture in the soup kettle with the browned flour and cook a minute further. Deglaze the pan with white wine, reduce by half. Add the crawfish stock and bring to a simmer. Allow to cook for 20 minutes and thicken. Meanwhile, combine the reserved crawfish in the bowl with the bread crumbs, herbs, and whipped egg whites. Mold into small squares or balls and place on a sheet pan. Spray with cooking spray and bake in the oven for 15 minutes. Skim any impurities from the bisque and adjust the seasoning. Serve bisque with rice and crawfish "croutons."

Fish Soup with Garlic and Escarole

4 lb. red snapper
1½ cups low-sodium vegetable broth
2 tbsp. rosemary, chopped
¼ cup olive oil
10 cloves garlic, mashed
1½ quarts onion, sliced
1 cup dry white wine
2 lb. red potatoes, cubed
1½ quarts low-sodium vegetable broth
1 head escarole, torn

This soup has the hearty soul of a soup, but is slightly delicate as well. For even better flavor, prepare your own vegetable broth. Place a quart of water with an onion, clove garlic, half tomato, and stalk of celery. Simmer for 20 minutes. Any mild white-flesh fish can be used. Just stay away from oily fish such as mackerel.
Serves 8

Place the red snapper in a soup pot with 1½ cups of broth and rosemary. Cover and steam 5 minutes or until just cooked through. Remove from the pot and reserve. Add oil to pan and sauté the onion on medium-low heat until translucent. Add the garlic, white wine, potatoes, and 1½ quarts broth. Bring to a boil, reduce heat, and simmer until potatoes are tender. Add the escarole and fish with juices and rosemary. Cook 5 minutes on a low simmer.

Calories (kcal)	*476*
Total Fat (gm)	*10*
% Calories from Fat	*20%*
Cholesterol (mg)	*84*
Sodium (mg)	*643*

Italian Bean and Pasta Soup

- 2 cups dry chickpeas, soaked overnight
- 1 tbsp. extra virgin olive oil
- 1 cup onion, sliced
- 1 cup dry white wine
- 1 cup penne pasta, cooked and drained
- 8 baguette slices, toasted
- 1 cup egg substitute
- 6 oz. mozzarella cheese, part skim milk, sliced
- 1/4 cup Parmesan cheese

This is a classic Italian soup traditionally called Zuppa alla Molisana, a fancy name for such a simple peasant-style dish. Served with a green salad it will make a complete meal.
Serves 8

Clean chickpeas, refresh water, and soak overnight. In a soup kettle, sauté the onions until translucent. Drain peas from the soaking water. Reserve water. Add chickpeas to pot and stir well. Add wine and 1 cup of reserved water. Bring to a boil and reduce by half. Add the pasta and turn off the heat.

Preheat oven to 375 degrees. Spray a baking dish with cooking pray. Dip bread slices in egg substitute and place a layer in the bottom of the pan. Add half the soup on top. Layer half the cheese slices. Add rest of soup, with a layer of mozzarella. Add 2 cups of the reserved soaking liquid and sprinkle with Parmesan. Bake in the oven for 30 minutes.

Calories (kcal)	*461*
Total Fat (gm)	*13*
% Calories from Fat	*27%*
Cholesterol (mg)	*14*
Sodium (mg)	*386*

Mexican Hominy Stew

1 lb. pork loin, finely chopped
Vegetable cooking spray
1 tbsp. garlic, minced
1 tbsp. chipotle pepper, minced
½ cup onion, chopped
¼ cup green bell pepper, chopped
5 cups hominy, yellow, canned and rinsed
1 can diced tomatoes
1 cup red wine
3 cups low-sodium beef broth
Salt and pepper, to taste
¼ cup cilantro, coarse chopped
¼ cup fat-free sour cream

Hominy, like beans, is available as a dried or a canned product. The canned product is really quite wonderful after being rinsed and drained. It is also convenient in helping to decrease cooking time. Hominy has a very mild, starchy flavor that will absorb the other flavors married with it. Here we accent with chipotle peppers, but any nice ground chili blend also works well. Hominy does have some roots in Mexican cuisine, but it is found mostly in Native American cuisine. It is delicious all the same.
Serves 6

Heat a medium sauce pan with vegetable cooking spray. Brown the chopped pork meat and remove from the pan. Add the garlic, chipotle, onion, and green bell pepper. Sauté for 5 minutes. Add the canned and rinsed hominy, tomatoes, wine, and beef broth. Bring to a simmer and cook for 30 minutes. Adjust seasoning with salt and pepper, and add the cilantro. Serve in bowls garnished with a dollop of sour cream. Consistency should be fairly thick.

Calories (kcal)	276
Total Fat (gm)	9
% Calories from Fat	30%
Cholesterol (mg)	39
Sodium (mg)	639

New England Clam Chowder

2 dozen clams, washed
¾ cup water
1 lemon, halved
Vegetable cooking spray
3 cups onion, chopped
1 tbsp. garlic, minced
1½ lb. russet potatoes, peeled and cubed
1 cup celery, chopped
½ cup lean ham, chopped
2 cups water
1 tbsp. thyme, chopped
1 bay leaf
3 tbsp. flour
2 cups low-fat 2% milk
Salt and pepper, to taste

A New England clam chowder is a white creamy-based clam chowder, while the Manhattan clam chowder is tomato based. Typically the New England clam chowder is loaded with fat and calories. Here is our tasty but healthy version. If fresh clams are not available, substitute 8 ounces of rinsed, drained canned clams with ½ cup bottled clam juice.
Serves 8

Place clams, water, and halved lemon in a soup kettle. Bring water to a boil, cover, and steam clams until they open. Drain, reserving the clam juice. Discard the lemon. Remove the clam meat from the shells and reserve.

Spray the soup pot with cooking spray, and sauté the onion and garlic for 2 minutes. Add the celery and ham, and sauté a further 2 minutes on medium heat. Add the potatoes and fold together, before adding the clam juice, water, thyme, and bay. Bring to a boil, reduce heat to a simmer, and cook for 20 minutes or until potatoes are tender. Season with salt and pepper.

Meanwhile, add the flour to the milk and stir into a slurry. When potatoes are tender, add the flour and milk mixture. Cook a further 15 minutes on medium heat. Do not boil or milk will separate. Add the clams and adjust the seasoning with salt and pepper if necessary.

Calories (kcal)	*138*
Total Fat (gm)	*2*
% Calories from Fat	*12%*
Cholesterol (mg)	*10*
Sodium (mg)	*180*

Potato and Leek Soup with Asiago Croutons

Vegetable cooking spray
1½ tsp. garlic, minced
2 leeks, cleaned and chopped
¾ cup white wine
1 quart chicken stock, or low-sodium broth
2 lb. red new potatoes, cut ½-inch thick
1 tbsp. fresh sage
2½ tbsp. Asiago cheese, grated
½ loaf sourdough bread, cubed
1 tsp. unsalted butter, melted
¼ cup Half and Half

You have an option to serve this soup in two ways. One is more homestyle, with large morsels of potatoes. The other is more classically French and smooth in texture. Both are delicious and low in fat. Using white wine in the soup enables the delicate aroma of leeks and sage rise to the occasion.
Serves 6

Spray a soup pot with cooking spray. Sauté the garlic and leeks until translucent. Deglaze with white wine. Add the cubed potatoes, sage, and chicken broth. Bring to a boil, reduce heat to a slow simmer, and cook for 30 minutes, or until potatoes are very tender. Adjust the seasoning, and remove from heat.

Toss Asiago cheese with bread cubes and melted butter. Toast in a 275-degree oven for 20 minutes. Before serving, fold Half and Half into soup and garnish with croutons. If you wish, mash some of the potatoes, or pass through a food mill for a smooth texture.

Calories (kcal)	*196*
Total Fat (gm)	*5*
% Calories from Fat	*24%*
Cholesterol (mg)	*11*
Sodium (mg)	*622*

Pumpkin Velouté

Vegetable cooking spray
2 cups onion, chopped
1 tbsp. garlic, minced
2 tbsp. ginger root, minced
2 lb. pumpkin puree
1 quart low-sodium chicken broth
Pinch allspice
Salt and pepper, to taste
1 cup pumpkin kernels, roasted

This is a smooth and silky soup to start any meal or to serve by itself. Serve with dark pumpernickel toasts spread with a soft goat's cheese as the perfect accompaniment.
Serves 8

Spray a soup kettle with cooking spray. Sauté the onion, garlic, and ginger root on medium-low heat for 5 minutes. Do not caramelize. Add the pumpkin puree, allspice, salt, and pepper. Cook 2 minutes, blending well. Add the chicken broth. Bring to a boil, reduce heat to a simmer, and cook for 20 minutes. Adjust the seasoning and consistency if necessary with salt, pepper, or chicken broth. Garnish with pumpkin kernels.

Calories (kcal)	230
Total Fat (gm)	12
% Calories from Fat	44%
Cholesterol (mg)	0
Sodium (mg)	272

Smoked Chicken and Okra Gumbo

¾ cup flour, browned
3 tbsp. tasso ham, minced
½ cup onion, chopped
2 tbsp. garlic, minced
¼ cup celery, chopped
¼ cup green bell pepper, chopped
¾ cup green onion, chopped
1 bay leaf
1 lb. chicken breast halves without skin, cubed

Any soup tastes fantastic when slowly cooked with a juicy ham bone. But a ham bone can have a lot of residual fat. Tasso ham is a wonderful smoked meat that is lower in fat. A small amount goes a long way, and it is packed with great flavor. Here it is used in a traditional Louisiana soup hearty enough for a complete meal.
Serves 6

In a medium soup pot, sauté the tasso, onion, and garlic for 3 minutes. Add the celery, bell pepper, green onion, and chicken. Continue to sauté until cooked through, about 7 minutes. Fold in the okra and sprinkle with flour. Mix until well combined. Add the stock and bring to a simmer. Cook for at least 1 hour in order for okra to thicken the soup. Add

1 lb. frozen okra, cut ½-inch thick
3 quarts chicken stock, or low-sodium broth
1 cup diced tomatoes, canned
4 cups cooked rice

the tomatoes and cook a further 10 minutes. Serve the gumbo over hot cooked rice.

Calories (kcal)	425
Total Fat (gm)	5
% Calories from Fat	10%
Cholesterol (mg)	37
Sodium (mg)	1717

Southwestern Chili

Vegetable cooking spray
1½ lb. ground turkey
2 tbsp. garlic, minced
1 cup onion, chopped
½ cup green Ancho pepper or bell pepper, chopped
½ cup red bell pepper
2 tbsp. chili powder
½ tsp. cumin
1 tbsp. orange zest
1 tsp. oregano, dried
3 cans canned tomatoes, diced
1 can black beans, rinsed and drained
1 can kidney beans, rinsed and drained
2 cups low-sodium beef broth
½ cup chopped cilantro, optional

Serve with corn bread, sliced mango, and avocado to complete a delicious meal.
Serves 12

Spray a medium sauce pan with vegetable cooking spray. Brown the ground turkey until opaque. Add the garlic, onion, green pepper, red bell pepper, chili powder, cumin, orange zest, and oregano. Sauté for 3 minutes, then add tomatoes, black beans, and kidney beans. Bring to a simmer and adjust the consistency of the chili with the beef broth. Cook for at least 30 minutes, stirring occasionally. Just before serving stir in the cilantro.

Calories (kcal)	218
Total Fat (gm)	6
% Calories from Fat	22%
Cholesterol (mg)	45
Sodium (mg)	305

Spinach, Oyster, and Artichoke Soup

1 artichoke
1 lemon, halved
2 pints oysters
Vegetable cooking spray
1 cup white onions, chopped
2 tsp. garlic, minced
¼ cup flour, all-purpose, browned
1 quart milk
3 tbsp. basil leaves, chopped
1 bunch fresh spinach, washed and chopped
¼ cup Parmesan cheese, grated
2 tbsp. Worcestershire sauce
½ tsp. paprika

Browned flour is used as a thickening agent in this soup. To brown the flour, place it in a clean, dry sauté pan on medium heat. Moving the flour around in the pan, cook until flour is a warm chestnut color. This is used in place of a high fat roux base. Feel free to brown flour and store in an airtight container in your pantry. It will hold for a month, if not longer.
Serves 12

Fill a medium sauce pan with 1 inch of water. Place the lemon halves in the water. Place the artichokes in a steamer basket in the sauce pan, and cover. Steam over medium-high heat until artichokes are just tender, about 35 minutes, depending on the size. Remove from steamer and allow to cool. Remove leaves from the artichoke and reserve. Scoop out the hairy choke found in the center of the heart and discard. Coarsely chop the heart and reserve. Strain the oysters from their liquid, reserving liquid.

Spray a soup pot with cooking spray. Heat pan to medium high, and sauté the onion and garlic. Add the artichoke heart, flour, and basil. Sauté an additional 2 minutes. Add the skim milk and the oyster liquid. Bring to a slow simmer, stirring until the soup thickens. Do not boil or it will separate. Add the spinach, cheese, and Worcestershire sauce. Just before serving, add the oysters to barely poach. Do not overcook oysters. To serve, ladle soup into bowls and garnish with paprika. Serve the leaves around the sides of the plates to dip into the soup.

Calories (kcal)	*134*
Total Fat (gm)	*5*
% Calories from Fat	*35%*
Cholesterol (mg)	*54*
Sodium (mg)	*325*

Vegetable Orecchiette Soup

½ cup andouille sausage, diced
½ cup onion, chopped
1 tbsp. garlic, chopped
¼ cup red bell pepper, chopped
¼ cup carrot, peeled and chopped
1 tbsp. thyme
1½ bay leaves
1 cup white wine
3 quarts low-sodium chicken broth
3 cups orecchiette pasta, or shell pasta
¼ cup cauliflower, chopped
¼ cup lima beans
¼ cup sweet corn, kernels
¼ cup broccoli, chopped
¼ cup peas
½ cup Swiss chard, chopped

Orecchiette is a wonderful pasta about the size of a thumb print . . . in fact, that's exactly what it is. The pasta is shaped by an indentation of a thumb print and resembles little "ears." It offers great texture and flavor for a special soup. If fresh vegetables are not available, use a frozen product. Try to stay away from canned vegetables. They are far too high in sodium, and the quality of nutrition, texture, and flavor is not up to par.
Serves 12

Put a large soup pot on low heat. Add the andouille sausage and cook slowly for 2 minutes. Add the onion, carrot, and garlic and cook for 2 more minutes. Add the thyme and bay. Fold together before adding the white wine. Cook 3 minutes, then add the chicken broth. Bring to a simmer. Add the pasta, cauliflower, lima beans, and corn. Cook about 20 minutes until pasta is tender, then add the broccoli, peas, and Swiss chard. Bring to a simmer, and cook a final 10 minutes.

Calories (kcal)	216
Total Fat (gm)	6
% Calories from Fat	27%
Cholesterol (mg)	7
Sodium (mg)	615

El Xochitl (Chicken Soup Fiesta)

1 whole chicken, skinned
1 chili pepper, dried
1 red onion, quartered
1 red bell pepper, split
1 stalk celery
1 bay leaf
1 gallon water
2 tsp. chili powder
1 tbsp. tomato paste
1 cup white rice, washed and drained
2 cups water
2 cups yellow sweet corn, cut off cob
1 tsp. garlic, minced
2 tbsp. green onion, chopped
2 cans black beans, rinsed and drained
½ can diced tomatoes, rinsed and drained
½ red bell pepper, julienne
¼ red onion, thinly sliced
½ cup cilantro, picked
1 cup cabbage, shredded
1 package small flour tortillas, warmed

For ease in preparation, these side dishes have been simplified. You can be even more creative by adding other items, such as seasoned avocado, jalapeno, pinto beans, garbanzo beans, or other festive additions. Be your own chef and have fun being creative with fresh ingredients.

Serves 12

In a large stock pot, combine the chicken, chili pepper, red onion, bell pepper, celery, bay, and water. Bring to a boil, reduce heat, and allow to simmer for 1½ hours. Meanwhile, sauté the rice, tomato paste, and chili powder in a sauce pan to combine. Add the water. Bring to a boil, reduce heat, cover, and cook 20 minutes. Sauté the corn and garlic on low heat with a splash of stock. Season with chopped green onion. Drain and rinse the black beans. Add ½ cup of stock and cook for 10 minutes. Fold in tomato and hold.

Cut the bell pepper and cabbage, and pick the cilantro. Cover the tortillas in foil or in a covered container and warm in a 350-degree oven for 10 minutes. Strain the broth into a clean soup pot. Pick the chicken from the bones. Discard other vegetables and spice from broth and keep broth hot.

To serve, place bowls of corn with green onion, black beans, rice, sliced vegetables, and tortillas in the center of the table. Spoon broth into bowls and evenly divide chicken into bowls. Each guest at the table is free to add ingredients to make his or her own original Xochitl soup. The tortillas may also be used to roll ingredients inside them.

Calories (kcal)	386
Total Fat (gm)	13
% Calories from Fat	30%
Cholesterol (mg)	70
Sodium (mg)	95

CHAPTER 5

Vegetarian

Black Bean-Stuffed Sweet Potatoes
Broiled Chiles Rellenos
Creole Stuffed Bell Peppers
Family-Style Ratatouille over Southern Corn Bread
Grilled Spring Vegetable Pizza
Grilled Tofu with Olive Tapenade and Preserved Lemons
Herbed Rice Cakes with Red Bean Sauce
Heritage Shepherd's Pie
Italian Vegetable Tart
Mushroom and Artichoke Pasta
Napa Cabbage and Mushroom Sauté
Stir-Fried Rice Noodles
Stuffed Peppers with Hominy Grits
Summer Squash with Shaved Romano
Sun-Dried Tomato and Vegetable Pizza
Vegetarian Pesto Lasagna

Black Bean-Stuffed Sweet Potatoes

3 sweet potatoes, or yams
2 cans black beans, rinsed and drained
Pinch of cumin
¼ jalapeno pepper, minced
1 cup water
½ cup canned tomatoes, diced and drained

This is great served alone or as a side dish to roast chicken or grilled fish for a Caribbean flair.
Serves 6

Pierce the potatoes with a fork and bake in a 350-degree oven for 45 minutes. An option is to microwave the potatoes for 10 minutes, turning after 5 minutes. Combine the black beans, cumin, jalapeno, and water in a small sauce pan. Bring to a simmer. Lower the heat and cook for 15 minutes. Add the tomatoes and cook another 5 minutes. Split the sweet potatoes in half, scrunch and fluff, and fill each half with black beans. This is great served alone or as a side dish to roast chicken or grilled fish for a Caribbean flair.

Calories (kcal)	274
Total Fat (gm)	1
% Calories from Fat	4%
Cholesterol (mg)	0
Sodium (mg)	43

Broiled Chiles Rellenos

8 poblano chile peppers
Vegetable cooking spray
1 acorn squash, peeled and seeded
1 tbsp. garlic, chopped
1 cup onion, chopped
½ cup red bell pepper, chopped
¼ tsp. cumin, ground
¼ tsp. cinnamon, ground
½ tsp. salt

A delicious southwestern-style dish. I usually roast one or two extra chiles in case one splits open.
Serves 8

Char chile peppers over a flame until all sides are blackened. Place in a bowl while they are still hot and cover. Allow to sit for 5 minutes to steam. Peel the skins from the chiles. Cut a slit lengthwise down the pepper. Remove the seeds, reserving the juices if you can. The roasted chile pepper will become a pocket stuffed with the acorn squash filling. Using a sharp knife, dice the squash into small cubes. In a medium skillet, sauté the garlic and onion on medium-high heat to caramelize. Add the red bell pepper, cumin, cinnamon, salt,

Vegetarian

1 tsp. cracked black pepper
½ cup low-sodium chicken broth
2 cups tomato salsa

and pepper. Fold the cubed squash to coat well, add chicken stock, and cover. Cook squash for 10 minutes or until tender. Fill each chile pepper with about ⅓ cup squash. Arrange chiles in a baking dish, cover with foil, and bake for 30 minutes. Serve with salsa.

Calories (kcal)	76
Total Fat (gm)	0.4
% Calories from Fat	4%
Cholesterol (mg)	0
Sodium (mg)	340

Creole Stuffed Bell Peppers

12 green, red, and yellow bell peppers
2 tbsp. olive oil
½ cup onion, chopped
1 tbsp. garlic, chopped
3 cups couscous
1 quart water
½ cup tomatoes, seeded and chopped
½ cup green onion, chopped
Salt and pepper, to taste

Talk about a simple recipe with great flavor! To many people, couscous is known as Moroccan pasta, but its roots also spread to African cuisine and Creole cuisine. Combined with the flavors of a Creole garden, this a sure to be a crowd pleaser. Serve with corn on the cob and fresh tomato salad for a delicious menu.
Serves 6

Cut the very top off the bell peppers with stem and scoop out the seeds, leaving a pepper "cup" to fill with stuffing. Chop the tops of the peppers from around the stem and reserve. Heat a medium sauce pan of olive oil. Sauté the onion and garlic for 3 minutes, or until evenly brown and caramelized. Add chopped bell pepper and couscous. Fold together and then add water or vegetable stock. Cover and cook for 5 minutes. Uncover and fold in the tomatoes and green onion. Season with salt and pepper. Fill bell peppers with stuffing. Place ⅔ cup water in the bottom of a baking pan, cover and bake at 350-degrees for 30 minutes. Serve 2 bell peppers per person.

Calories (kcal)	436
Total Fat (gm)	6
% Calories from Fat	11%
Cholesterol (mg)	0
Sodium (mg)	69

Family-Style Ratatouille over Southern Corn Bread

1 tsp. olive oil
1 tbsp. garlic, minced
¼ cup onion, chopped
1 each carrot, peeled and chopped
½ each red bell pepper, seeded and chopped
1½ cups eggplant, diced with skin
2 cans diced tomatoes, drained
¼ cup green onion, sliced
1 sprig fresh rosemary
Cracked black pepper, to taste
Kosher salt, to taste
¼ oz. Parmesan cheese, shaved in sheets
6 pieces corn bread

This ratatouille is much like an eggplant camponata. Its rich, warm personality is great on a chilly evening.
Serves 6

In a medium-sized sauce pan, sauté the onion and garlic in the olive oil for 1 minute. Add the carrot and sauté 1 more minute. Next, add the bell pepper and the eggplant, and sauté for 2 minutes. Add the drained tomatoes and rosemary, and season with salt and pepper. Stir and allow to simmer for 15 minutes. Before serving, add the green onion and adjust the seasoning with salt and pepper to your taste. If you are watching your sodium intake, please do not add any more salt. Serve in a bowl over hot corn bread, and shave a little Parmesan on top with a vegetable peeler.

Calories (kcal)	222
Total Fat (gm)	7
% Calories from Fat	27%
Cholesterol (mg)	38
Sodium (mg)	524

Grilled Spring Vegetable Pizza

1 cup warm water
1 package active dry yeast
1 tbsp. garlic, minced
1 tbsp. extra virgin olive oil
½ tsp. kosher salt
3 cups flour
1 zucchini, sliced lengthwise
2 cups shiitake mushrooms, stemmed

A great menu item for a party. Guests enjoy standing around the barbecue and watching the pizza dough crisp in front of their eyes.
Serves 6

Proof the yeast in the warm water. Knead the yeast, oil, and flour together. Allow to rise in a warm space until double in size. Knead in garlic, and cut into 1-cup portions. Set aside. Prepare a hot grill, and grill the zucchini, mushrooms, eggplant, and onion. Remove from grill. Roll each dough ball into a circle. Turn in your hands like you are turning the wheel of a car. The weight of the dough will shape into a uniform disc.

Vegetarian

2 tomatoes, sliced thin
½ red onion, sliced thin
1 cup mozzarella cheese, part skim milk, grated
¼ cup Romano cheese, grated
¼ cup Greek olives, pitted
4 cups baby lettuce leaves
2 tsp. lemon juice
1 tsp. extra virgin olive oil
Salt and pepper, to taste

Place directly on the grill grate. Grill until one side is crispy. Turn, and decoratively place vegetables on pizza and sprinkle with cheeses. Once cooked on that side, remove from grill. To garnish with further flavor, toss the greens, lemon, and olive oil, and season with salt and pepper. Place greens on top of pizza, cut, and serve.

Calories (kcal)	*456*
Total Fat (gm)	*11*
% Calories from Fat	*21%*
Cholesterol (mg)	*15*
Sodium (mg)	*489*

Grilled Tofu with Olive Tapenade and Preserved Lemons

2 tofu blocks, extra firm
Vegetable cooking spray
¼ cup Greek olives, pitted
2 tbsp. fresh herbs
1 tsp. anchovy fillets
1 tbsp. garlic, minced
2 tbsp. tomato, seeded and chopped
3 lemons
2 cups water
½ cup sugar
⅓ cup kosher salt
2 tbsp. ground black pepper

Small appetizers served for a Spanish menu are known as "tapas." This is a delicious vegetarian tapa you are sure to enjoy.
Serves 4

Preheat an oven to 350 degrees. Slice tofu ¼-inch thick, lay on towels to absorb moisture, and place in the cooler. With a mortar and pestle (or mini food chopper), blend the olives, herbs, garlic, and anchovies. Lightly fold the tomato into black olive mixture. With a knife, peel the lemons and remove as much of the pith as possible. Slice rind thin. In a small sauce pan, bring the sugar and water to a boil and lower heat to a simmer. Add the lemons and cook for 10 minutes on low heat. Combine salt and pepper. Drain the lemon peel and lay in salt and pepper tossing to coat. Allow to dry. This can be done ahead of time and held in an airtight container. Spray a sheet pan with cooking spray and lay tofu slices on pan. Bake in the oven for 15 minutes. Spread the baked tofu with olive tapenade and garnish with lemon peels.

Calories (kcal)	*178*
Total Fat (gm)	*7*
% Calories from Fat	*30%*
Cholesterol (mg)	*1*
Sodium (mg)	*1094*

Herbed Rice Cakes with Red Bean Sauce

4 cups cooked white rice, sticky
2 tbsp. mixed herbs
Salt and pepper, to taste
2 tbsp. corn oil
1½ cups red beans
½ cup onion, chopped
1 tbsp. garlic, chopped
Pinch cumin seed, toasted
6 cups spinach, washed and picked
1 Roma tomato, seeded and chopped

Calories (kcal)	387
Total Fat (gm)	6
% Calories from Fat	13%
Cholesterol (mg)	0
Sodium (mg)	97

This dish can be served any time of the year, and thus the herbs used should be those that are fresh and available at the time. To combine your own fresh herb blend, decide on 3 or 4 herbs with distinct flavor—for example, thyme, sage, rosemary, and oregano. Chop equal amounts of each and fold together. Chop an amount of fresh parsley equal to the whole amount of blended herbs just chopped. Parsley is a noncompetitive, pure herbaceous flavor to marry all of the flavors. Add a bit of lemon zest for clean flavor, and you have a great herb blend. A covered jar will keep it fresh in the refrigerator for days on end, available to be added to all dishes throughout the week.
Serves 6

Mix the cooked rice with fresh herbs, and season with salt and pepper. Mold into 12 rice patties and place in the cooler to chill. In a small sauce pan, combine the beans, garlic, and onions. Cover with water 1 inch over beans. Bring to a slow simmer and cook beans until tender, about 10 minutes. Puree beans in a food processor until smooth, place back into pot, and adjust any seasonings. Heat a medium sauté pan of corn oil. Sauté the rice cakes until browned on both sides and heated through. Remove from the pan, and add the spinach with a splash of water to wilt. Serve the cakes with greens and sauce. Sprinkle with chopped tomato to garnish.

Heritage Shepherd's Pie

1 cup onion, chopped
2 tbsp. garlic, chopped
2 cups mushrooms, chopped
½ cup carrot, chopped
½ cup celery, chopped
3 tbsp. fresh herbs, chopped
1 small eggplant, cubed
2 cups tomatoes, canned, diced and drained
5 Idaho potatoes, peeled and cubed
½ cup milk, scalded
2 tbsp. unsalted butter, melted
1 tbsp. Parmesan cheese, grated

Shepherd's pie is a great English tradition, along with its counterpart, cottage pie. Cottage pie encloses its filling with a buttery crust that is much higher in fat and calories. Here we utilize flavors taken from fresh vegetables and potatoes, giving us a fantastic family dish or easy dinner party entree perfect for today's lifestyles.
Serves 6

Spray the bottom of a 2-quart casserole pan with cooking spray and preheat an oven to 375 degrees. Sauté onion and garlic for 1 minute. Add the chopped mushrooms and cook for 5 minutes. You want to remove as much moisture from the mushrooms as possible. Add the carrot and celery and cook 1 more minute. Add 1 tbsp. of the herbs, eggplant, and tomato. Cook for 20 minutes at a slow simmer. Steam the potatoes tender, about 5 minutes. Mash and fold with hot milk and melted butter. Add the remaining 2 tbsp. of herbs and Parmesan cheese. Season potatoes with salt and pepper. Layer the vegetables on bottom of casserole, layer potatoes on top. Place in oven and bake for 15-20 minutes.

Calories (kcal)	165
Total Fat (g)	6
% Calories from Fat	29%
Cholesterol (mg)	14
Sodium (mg)	279

Italian Vegetable Tart

4 oz. non-fat cream cheese
2 oz. margarine, half stick
1¼ cups flour
Pinch salt
1 tbsp. chives, minced
⅔ cup Calamata olives, pitted and chopped
2 anchovy fillets
1 tbsp. capers
5 Roma tomatoes, thinly sliced
1 tbsp. garlic, chopped
2 zucchini, shredded
Salt and pepper, to taste
½ cup basil leaves

Calories (kcal)	159
Total Fat (gm)	7
% Calories from Fat	36%
Cholesterol (mg)	2
Sodium (mg)	198

To complete a great vegetarian meal, serve with cooked white beans seasoned with sage, and fresh melon wedges.
Serves 8

In a food processor, blend the cream cheese and margarine. Add the flour and salt and process until dough forms a ball. Turn out onto a clean working surface. Knead the chives into the dough and form into a hockey puck shape. Place in refrigerator to chill completely. Roll out dough into a thin sheet. Place into a 9-inch tart round with removable bottom. Allow dough to fall over edges of the pan and cut off as a clean edge. Line with foil or paper and weigh pastry with pastry weights or uncooked rice. Bake in a 350-degree oven for 10 minutes. Remove weights and continue cooking for 15 minutes.

Meanwhile, combine the olives, anchovies, and capers in a bowl. Mix well, mashing ingredients together with the back of a wooden spoon. In a sauté pan, sauté the garlic and zucchini for 3 minutes. Remove, season with salt and pepper, and allow to cool.

To assemble, spread the olive mixture on the bottom of tart. Layer tomatoes over olives. Layer zucchini on top of tomatoes. Garnish with basil and serve at room temperature.

Mushroom and Artichoke Pasta

14 oz. artichoke hearts, canned in brine
3 tbsp. extra virgin olive oil
1 lb. mushrooms, quartered
1 tbsp. garlic, minced
4 cups low-sodium chicken broth
1 tbsp. fresh thyme

The delicate ribbons of egg noodles give this dish a special Central European feel. Great idea for a luncheon—just toss pasta at the last moment before serving.
Serves 8

Rinse and drain artichokes well. Slice into small bite-sized pieces. Heat a large pot of boiling salted water. Cook pasta until tender and drain.

Salt, to taste
½ lb. frozen chopped spinach, defrosted
12 oz. egg noodles
⅔ cup Parmesan cheese, grated
¼ cup parsley, chopped
Cracked black pepper

In a large sauté pan, heat olive oil. Sauté the mushrooms with the garlic, about 2 minutes. Add the artichoke hearts and sauté a further minute. Add the broth, thyme, and salt to taste. Bring to a simmer and cook 10 minutes. Add the spinach, pasta, Parmesan, parsley, and pepper. Toss well and serve.

Calories (kcal)	312
Total Fat (gm)	9
% Calories from Fat	26%
Cholesterol (mg)	46
Sodium (mg)	466

Napa Cabbage and Mushroom Sauté

1 tofu cake, sliced
1 tsp. salt
Vegetable cooking spray
1 tbsp. garlic, minced
2 tbsp. ginger root, minced
1 head Napa cabbage, sliced
1 cup red bell pepper, julienne
2 tbsp. soy sauce
2 tbsp. rice wine vinegar
½ tsp. sesame oil
2 cups oriental mushrooms
¼ cup green onion, chopped
3 tbsp. cilantro, chopped
1 package eggroll skins, chopped and baked

Although tofu has been a shining star in cuisine for centuries, longer than the history of our nation, it is a wonderful ingredient that more Americans should become familiar with. It provides great nutrition, but also gives our fast-paced lives quick and easy meals with great diversity for everyday. Another great soy product is tempeh, which can be substituted in this recipe.
Serves 6

In a bowl, combine the soy sauce, rice wine vinegar, and sesame oil. Slice the tofu about ½-inch thick, and marinate in sauce. Heat a wok or sauté pan with cooking spray. Add the ginger root and garlic and cook 1 minute. Add the cabbage and peppers and cook another 2 minutes. Pour off some of the marinade, about 3 tbsp., into pan and simmer or stir-fry 2 minutes and remove onto a plate or platter. Spray the pan again and pan-sear the tofu until crispy on the outside and warmed through. Remove onto the cabbage. Add the mushrooms and the rest of marinade. Stir-fry on low so that some of the mushroom juices are released. Add the scallions and cilantro. Toss in pan lightly before removing to top off the tofu. Garnish with fried or baked eggroll wrappers.

Calories (kcal)	94
Total Fat (gm)	3
% Calories from Fat	27%
Cholesterol (mg)	0
Sodium (mg)	669

Stir-Fried Rice Noodles

½ lb. rice-stick noodles
2 cups carrots, julienned
3 cups broccoli florets
2 cups leeks, julienned
1 cup red onion, sliced
½ cup low-sodium chicken broth
1 tsp. cornstarch
4 tbsp. soy sauce
1 tbsp. sugar
1 tsp. salt
1 tsp. sesame oil
2 tsp. canola oil
2 tsp. garlic, minced
2 tbsp. ginger root, minced
1 tbsp. curry powder
½ tsp. turmeric
½ cup green onion, julienned

The trick to any wok cookery is to have all of your ingredients ready before you turn on the heat. A great garnish to this dish is baked won ton wrappers. Place wrappers on a sheet pan and bake at 350 degrees until brown and crispy (about 5 minutes). Serve with Pickled Vegetables (see recipe) to complete the menu.
Serves 8

In a large bowl, soak noodles in boiling water for 5 minutes or until tender. Drain. Lightly blanch the carrots, broccoli, and leeks. Set aside with red onion. In a bowl, stir together the chicken broth, cornstarch, soy sauce, sugar, salt, and sesame oil.

Heat a wok with canola oil until very hot. Stir-fry the garlic and ginger root 1 minute. Add curry powder and turmeric and stir-fry until the aroma rises. Add sauce ingredients. Bring to a boil and allow to thicken slightly. Toss in noodles, vegetables, and green onion. Serve.

Calories (kcal)	81
Total Fat (gm)	2
% Calories from Fat	22%
Cholesterol (mg)	0
Sodium (mg)	835

Stuffed Peppers with Hominy Grits

8 red bell peppers
1 cup yellow grits
½ jalapeno chile pepper, minced
2 tsp. garlic powder
3½ cups water
½ tsp. salt

Serve these stuffed peppers as a delicious vegetarian dish for dinner or even brunch.
Serves 8

Remove the tops from the peppers and scoop out the seeds, leaving cup-shaped peppers. If peppers are not cup shaped, and have a longer shape, set peppers on their sides and cut an opening to fill. Preheat an oven to 375 degrees.

2 cups frozen corn kernels, defrosted
6 oz. Monterey Jack cheese

Place the grits, jalapeno pepper, garlic powder, water, and salt in a sauce pan. Bring to a boil, stirring constantly. Reduce heat and simmer for 10 minutes. Fold corn into grits. Fill peppers with grits and allow to cool completely. Sprinkle with cheese, and bake in the oven for 20 minutes.

Calories (kcal)	211
Total Fat (gm)	7
% Calories from Fat	29%
Cholesterol (mg)	19
Sodium (mg)	254

Summer Squash with Shaved Romano

2 lb. zucchini
2 tsp. salt
1 tbsp. extra virgin olive oil
2 tbsp. garlic, minced
¾ cup green onion, thinly sliced
2 tbsp. water
4 tbsp. basil, coarsely chopped
2 medium eggplants, sliced 1 inch thick
1 tbsp. extra virgin olive oil
Cracked black pepper
½ cup Romano cheese, shaved

Serve two eggplant medallions as an entrée or one as a delightful appetizer.
Serves 8

Trim zucchini and then grate with the largest side of the grater. Combine with the salt and let sit 20 minutes on paper towels. Rinse thoroughly and dry with paper towels. Heat a sauté pan with olive oil and sauté the green onion, garlic, and water for 2 minutes. Turn off heat and fold zucchini with green onion mixture, and season with salt and pepper.

Preheat an oven to 375 degrees. Rub a sheet pan with 1 tbsp. of olive oil and lay eggplant on pan. Season with cracked black pepper. Bake in the oven for 15 minutes, or until centers are starting to break down. Top each eggplant medallion with zucchini, then with shaved Romano.

Calories (kcal)	116
Total Fat (gm)	6
% Calories from Fat	41%
Cholesterol (mg)	7
Sodium (mg)	627

Sun-Dried Tomato and Vegetable Pizza

1 pizza crust
½ eggplant, diced
½ fennel bulb, sliced
1 cup mushroom, sliced
Cracked black pepper
1 tbsp. extra virgin olive oil
½ cup Sun-Dried Tomato Pesto, see recipe
¾ cup Mozzarella cheese, part skim milk, grated
⅔ cup basil, chiffonade

When you roast the anise-flavored fennel, woodsy mushrooms, and eggplant together, the flavors permeate each other, giving a fabulous earthy flavor to this pizza.
Serves 8

Preheat an oven to 375 degrees. Prepare fresh pizza dough or purchase a pre-cooked one from the store. In a bowl, toss the diced eggplant, fennel, and mushrooms with olive oil and season with cracked black pepper. Place on a sheet pan, cover with foil, and roast in an oven for 15 minutes. Spread pesto on bottom of a pizza round. Arrange roasted vegetables on pizza and top with cheese. Bake in an oven set at 400 degrees for 10 minutes. Cut and garnish with basil.

Calories (kcal)	245
Total Fat (gm)	6
% Calories from Fat	23%
Cholesterol (mg)	6
Sodium (mg)	550

Vegetarian Pesto Lasagna

- 2 packages lasagna noodles, cooked and drained
- 2 lb. ricotta cheese, part skim milk
- 2 egg whites
- Salt and pepper, to taste
- 1 bunch spinach, washed and chopped
- 5 carrots, diced and blanched
- 2 zucchini, sliced
- 1 pint mushrooms, sliced
- 1 cup red bell pepper, chopped
- 12 Roma tomatoes, sliced
- 1 cup basil
- ¼ cup chives, chopped
- ½ cup parsley, picked
- 2 tbsp. extra virgin olive oil
- ¼ cup vegetable stock
- 2 tbsp. lemon juice
- Salt and pepper, to taste
- ⅛ cup Parmesan cheese, grated
- 4½ cups Marinara Sauce, recipe found in book

The recipe works great using the no-cook lasagna noodles. The pasta has a much more delicate texture and requires no pre-cooking of the noodles. Rather than layering pre-cooked noodles, lay raw noodles in the lasagna pan, and layer according to the recipe. Cover the lasagna with aluminum foil and bake for 35 minutes. Remove foil and continue baking the remaining 10 minutes.
Serves 12

In a bowl, combine the ricotta cheese and egg whites, and season with salt and pepper. In a food processor, puree the basil, chives, parsley, olive oil, lemon, and vegetable stock. Place in a bowl and mix with the mushrooms, carrots, zucchini, and red bell pepper. Season with salt and pepper to taste. In an 8-by-11-inch baking pan or lasagna pan, place a layer of cooked lasagna noodles. Next, place a layer of pesto vegetables on top. Cover with a second layer of noodles, then dot with a thin layer of ricotta cheese mixture. Then place a layer of spinach and a layer of tomato slices. Cover with another layer of pasta. Repeat this 4-layer procedure, finishing with pasta. Sprinkle with Parmesan. Bake the lasagna for 45 minutes. Allow to cool at least 10 minutes before slicing. Serve lasagna with Marinara Sauce.

Calories (kcal)	*330*
Total Fat (gm)	*13*
% Calories from Fat	*33%*
Cholesterol (mg)	*24*
Sodium (mg)	*781*

CHAPTER 6

Chicken and Poultry

Basil Chicken
Cane-Glazed Chicken Breasts with Leeks and Carrots
Chicken and Black Bean Quesadillas
Chicken and Chive Dumplings
Chicken and Sausage Jambalaya
Chicken Anise
Chicken Curry
Chicken Roulade with Asparagus and Prosciutto
Chicken with Blue Cheese Apples
Chicken with White Beans
Creole Roasted Cornish Hens
Duck and Sausage Cassoulet
Duck Breast with Grilled Radicchio and Sweet Bourbon Oranges
Holiday Turkey with Peppered Dressing
Lime-Marinated Emu Fajitas with Pumpkin Seeds
Pollo Spanish Rice
Simple Szechuan Stir-Fry
Tandoori Chicken

Basil Chicken

- 1½ lb. skinless, boneless chicken breast
- ½ tsp. salt
- 1 tsp. cracked black pepper
- 2 tsp. extra virgin olive oil
- 1 tbsp. flour
- 1 red bell pepper, medium diced
- 1 tsp. onion, chopped
- 1½ tsp. garlic
- ¾ cup basil, fresh
- ½ cup dry sherry
- ½ cup chicken stock, or low-sodium broth

Sherry is a great wine to use for all cooking. Make sure to use dry sherry, because sweet sherry will give foods a strong musky aroma. Fresh basil is a must for this recipe, but fresh parsley can be substituted.
Serves 6

Season chicken with salt and pepper. Heat a sauté pan with olive oil. Gently cook the chicken a golden brown. Sprinkle with flour and cook another 1 minute. Remove from the pan and add the sherry. Cook for 1 minute before adding the red bell pepper, onion, garlic, and chicken broth. Cook for 2 minutes at a steady simmer. Add the chicken back to the pan, cook 2 minutes, then wilt the basil over the chicken and fold together.

Calories (kcal)	180
Total Fat (gm)	4
% Calories from Fat	21%
Cholesterol (mg)	66
Sodium (mg)	324

Cane-Glazed Chicken Breasts with Leeks and Carrots

- 6 skinless chicken breasts
- ¼ cup cane syrup
- 3 tbsp. apple cider vinegar
- 1 tbsp. garlic, minced
- ½ cup Granny Smith apples, mashed
- 1 tbsp. ginger root, minced
- 1 tbsp. lemon juice
- 2 cups leeks, sliced ¼-inch thick
- 3 cups carrots, sliced ⅛-inch thick

Cane syrup has a rich flavor with a slight burnt aroma. If cane syrup is not available, substitute with dark brown sugar or cane sugar. By cooking the chicken on the bone, you add even more flavor. The meaty part of poultry, meats, and fish has much less flavor than the bones—a good rule to remember when trying to intensify flavor.
Serves 6

Combine the cane syrup, vinegar, garlic, mashed apples, ginger root, and lemon juice. Season with salt and pepper. Toss 3 tbsp. of cane mixture with carrots and leeks. Place on a sheet pan, cover with aluminum foil, and bake in a 350-degree oven for 20 minutes, or until carrots are tender. Toss the remaining cane mixture with chicken breasts and allow

Chicken and Poultry

Salt and pepper, to taste
1 bunch thyme, picked clean

to marinate at least 25 minutes. Place on a sheet pan and roast in oven for 35 minutes or until cooked through, being careful not to overcook. Serve roast chicken breasts with carrots and leeks and sprinkle with thyme leaves.

Calories (kcal)	324
Total Fat (gm)	3
% Calories from Fat	8%
Cholesterol (mg)	130
Sodium (mg)	180

Chicken and Black Bean Quesadillas

2 each chicken breast halves without skin, thinly sliced
1 tbsp. chili powder, ground
2 tsp. orange zest
1 can black beans, rinsed and drained
¼ cup green onions, sliced
1 cup Monterey Jack cheese, shredded
12 each flour tortillas
Vegetable cooking spray
½ avocado, pitted, skinned, sliced
1 cup salsa

A quick and easy menu that the whole family will enjoy. Make sure to rinse the black beans. For even better flavor, cook black beans fresh.
Serves 8

Season the chicken with chili and orange zest. Sauté or broil until cooked through, about 4 to 5 minutes. Heat a large sauté pan or griddle and spray with vegetable cooking spray. Place 1 tortilla in the pan. Add 1 tbsp. of cooked chicken, 1 tbsp. of black beans, 3 tbsp. of cheese, and 2 tsp. of green onion. Cover with a second tortilla like a girdled sandwich. Slowly heat for 2 to 3 minutes. With a spatula, turn and heat for another 2 to 3 minutes. Cut into wedges and serve with avocado and salsa.

Calories (kcal)	491
Total Fat (gm)	15
% Calories from Fat	28%
Cholesterol (mg)	39
Sodium (mg)	507

Chicken and Chive Dumplings

2½ lb. chicken breast halves without skin, cubed 2-inch pieces
Vegetable cooking spray
1 cup onion, chopped
½ cup carrot, chopped
½ cup celery, chopped
2 tbsp. garlic, minced
1 cup new potatoes, cubed ½-inch pieces
½ cup flour
1 quart chicken stock, low-sodium broth
¾ cup green peas, defrosted
1 cup biscuit dough, low-fat
3 tbsp. chives
1 tsp. cracked black pepper
Salt, to taste

This will freeze wonderfully. Prepare without dumplings and peas before freezing. The dumplings are actually crispy drop biscuits, deliciously light, and should be added just before serving. A great dish to have on hand for a lunch, dinner, or even Sunday brunch.
Serves 6

Heat medium sauté pan with vegetable cooking spray and sear the chicken breast cubes. Remove from pan and add the onion and garlic. Sauté until translucent, add the carrots, and cook 1 minute. Add the celery and potatoes, and cook a further minute. Add the chicken back to the pan, sprinkle with flour. Stir until vegetables and chicken are coated with flour. Add the chicken stock, and stir until it is well combined and comes to a simmer.

Cook on medium heat until the potatoes are tender. Meanwhile, mix the chives and pepper blend with the biscuit dough. Using any low-fat biscuit mix is convenient and easy. Drop 2 tbsp. of dough on a sheet pan, and bake in a preheated 400-degree oven for 3 minutes. To finish the recipe, add the green peas and baked dumplings to the chicken stew no more than 5 minutes before serving. Adjust seasoning with salt if desired.

Calories (kcal)	350
Total Fat (gm)	4
% Calories from Fat	12%
Cholesterol (mg)	88
Sodium (mg)	1108

Chicken and Sausage Jambalaya

Vegetable cooking spray
1½ tbsp. garlic, chopped
1½ cups onion, chopped
1 cup celery, chopped
¾ cup bell pepper

The historical roots of jambalaya reach into Spanish, French, and Caribbean cuisine. Like a hunter's stew, it should be made with whatever meats and vegetables are on hand. For today's lifestyles, these ingredients are always readily available at your local grocery. To reduce the sodium, use fresh tomatoes and omit the salt.
Serves 6

Chicken and Poultry 89

1½ lb. chicken breast halves without skin, diced 1 inch
6 oz. turkey sausage, sliced
1 tsp. thyme
1 tsp. sage
Pinch cumin
Salt, to taste
1 tsp. cracked black pepper
1¼ cups converted rice
¾ cup canned tomatoes, diced and drained
1¼ cups low-sodium beef broth
⅓ cup green onion, chopped

Spray a large pan with vegetable cooking spray and heat on medium-high heat. Sauté the garlic and onion until brown and caramelized. Add the celery and bell pepper and cook a minute. Next, add the chicken, sausage, thyme, sage, cumin, salt, and pepper. Cook until brown and rich in color. Add the rice and tomato, stir, then add beef broth. Bring to a rapid simmer, cover, and lower heat. Cook for 25 minutes. Remove cover and fluff with a spoon. Fold in green onions and serve.

Calories (kcal)	*329*
Total Fat (gm)	*6*
% Calories from Fat	*15%*
Cholesterol (mg)	*76*
Sodium (mg)	*668*

Chicken Anise

6 boned and skinned chicken breasts
1 tsp. anise seed
½ tsp. salt
Pepper, to taste
½ cup sour cream
¼ cup skim milk
2 tbsp. lemon juice
2 tbsp. fennel, chopped
Vegetable cooking spray

For a simple and quick mid-week meal. If the fresh fennel is not available, substitute dill.
Serves 6

Season chicken breasts with salt, pepper, and anise seed. In a bowl, combine the sour cream, milk, lemon, and fennel. Let sit and come to room temperature. Heat a medium sauté pan with vegetable cooking spray. Sauté one side of chicken, turn, and cover. Allow to cook through, about 5 minutes. Remove from the pan, and top with the fennel cream sauce.

Calories (kcal)	*237*
Total Fat (gm)	*7*
% Calories from Fat	*27%*
Cholesterol (mg)	*105*
Sodium (mg)	*307*

Chicken Curry

2 tsp. cornstarch
2½ cups non-fat buttermilk
1½ tbsp. curry powder
2 tsp. cumin, ground
Salt, to taste
2 lb. chicken tenders
1 lb. carrots, large julienned
2 tsp. canola oil
2 tbsp. shallot, minced
2 tbsp. garlic, minced
2 tbsp. ginger root, minced
½ tsp. crushed red pepper
3 bunches fresh spinach, rinsed
2 quarts cooked brown rice

I prefer using chicken tenders rather than chicken breasts for this recipe. They seem to maintain better moisture and flavor. If time permits, remove the tendon from the tenders. You do this by scraping and pulling the tendon with the back of a knife—like skinning a fish.
Serves 8

In a small bowl, dissolve the cornstarch into the buttermilk. Add the curry powder, cumin, and salt. Add the chicken tenders and stir to coat. Allow to marinate in the refrigerator for 1-2 hours.

Blanch the carrots in hot boiling water, drain and reserve. In a large skillet, heat canola oil. Sauté the shallot, garlic, and ginger root for 2 minutes. Add the marinated chicken tenders with marinade and cook for 5 minutes. Add the red pepper and spinach. Allow spinach to wilt. Adjust seasoning if necessary. Serve over hot steamed brown rice.

Calories (kcal)	*396*
Total Fat (gm)	*5*
% Calories from Fat	*11%*
Cholesterol (mg)	*66*
Sodium (mg)	*113*

Chicken Roulade with Asparagus and Prosciutto

3 lb. chicken breast halves without skin, trimmed of fat
Salt and pepper, to taste
¼ lb. prosciutto, thinly sliced
½ lb. Mozzarella cheese, part skim milk, sliced

A beautiful presentation and oh, so easy to make. Serve with seasoned carrots and a moist starch side dish, such as Peppered Spoon Bread (see page 161).
Serves 8

Pound the chicken breasts with a flat mallet to a uniform thickness. Season both sides with salt and pepper. Place the presentation side down on a clean working surface. Place a small slice of prosciutto on the breast. Next, lay a slice of

1 lb. asparagus, blanched
Vegetable cooking spray

Calories (kcal)	264
Total Fat (gm)	8
% Calories from Fat	28%
Cholesterol (mg)	104
Sodium (mg)	621

Mozzarella and then 3 spears of asparagus with tips protruding out one end slightly. Roll and tie with butcher's twine or hold with long toothpicks. Repeat the process for remaining chicken breasts.

Heat a large sauté pan with vegetable cooking spray. Sauté the chicken roulades on all sides, about 10 minutes, on medium heat until browned. Place in oven for 10 minutes to finish heating through. Serve 1 roulade per person, and slice each into 4 pieces about an inch thick.

Chicken with Blue Cheese Apples

6 chicken breast halves without skin
Salt and pepper, to taste
1 tsp. canola oil
1½ cups chicken stock, or low-sodium broth
¼ cup apple cider vinegar
1 tsp. garlic, minced
1 tbsp. honey
2 Granny Smith apples, cubed
3 oz. blue cheese, crumbled
1 tbsp. chives, minced

The sauce should resemble a creamy apple sauce that barely covers the back of a spoon. Wonderful served with brown rice and steamed spinach.
Serves 6

Season chicken breasts with salt and pepper. Heat a medium sauté pan with canola oil until hot. Sear the presentation side down and cook until golden brown. Turn over, cover, and finish cooking for 5 minutes or until cooked through. Uncover and remove the breasts. Add the vinegar and garlic and reduce to half. Add the stock, honey, and apples and cook for 8 to 10 minutes at a simmer. Lightly melt the blue cheese in the sauce, then spoon over chicken breasts. Garnish with chives.

Calories (kcal)	216
Total Fat (gm)	6
% Calories from Fat	23%
Cholesterol (mg)	76
Sodium (mg)	466

Chicken with White Beans

2 lb. chicken breast halves without skin, trimmed
½ tsp. lemon zest
1 tbsp. basil, fresh, chopped
1 tsp. kosher salt
Vegetable cooking spray
1 cup onion, chopped
½ cup carrot, chopped
½ cup celery, chopped
3 cups white beans, washed and picked
1 bouquet garni
6 cups chicken stock, or low-sodium broth
½ cup Italian parsley, coarse chopped
1 tbsp. oregano, coarse chopped
2 tbsp. basil, coarse chopped
2 tbsp. thyme, coarse chopped
1 tbsp. chives, coarse chopped
1 tbsp. sage, chopped
1 tbsp. rosemary, minced
1 tbsp. lemon zest
¼ cup extra virgin olive oil
¼ cup water

A typical bouquet will have a bay leaf, black peppercorns, a clove, and fresh parsley stems. Stems from the basil, and sage are also wonderful, but stay away from woody stems such as rosemary and brittle thyme, which can be bitter. Tie together inside a cheesecloth. The flavors here rely heavily on herbaceous flavor. The aromas are delightful.
Serves 6

Season the chicken breasts with zest, basil, and salt. Place in refrigerator. Prepare the bouquet garni in a cheesecloth with your favorite flavors. In a medium sauce pan, sauté the onion and carrot with vegetable cooking spray until tender. Add the celery, sauté 1 more minute, then add the beans. Cover beans with stock, add the bouquet garni, and bring to a simmer. Cook beans until tender but still firm to the tooth, about 45 minutes.

Meanwhile, chop the herbs separately and place in a food processor or blender. Add the zest, olive oil, and water. Puree until a smooth, emulsified texture is achieved. Heat a sauté pan or grill until very hot. Sear the chicken breasts on both sides until breast is just cooked through. Do not overcook. To serve, place a layer of beans on a plate, top with the chicken, then drizzle the salsa verde over the meat.

Calories (kcal)	*618*
Total Fat (gm)	*13*
% Calories from Fat	*19%*
Cholesterol (mg)	*70*
Sodium (mg)	*1301*

Creole Roasted Cornish Hens

- 3 lb. skinless Cornish game hens, split, trimmed
- 3 sun-dried tomatoes, minced fine
- 2 tbsp. onion flakes
- 1 tbsp. chives, freeze dried
- 2 tsp. garlic, minced, dry
- 1 tbsp. celery flakes
- 1 tbsp. lemon zest
- Vegetable cooking spray

Calories (kcal)	278
Total Fat (gm)	7
% Calories from Fat	21%
Cholesterol (mg)	91
Sodium (mg)	697

Few herbs are used in Creole seasoning. It should resemble flavors of a Creole garden full of tomatoes, scallions, onions, and garlic. By using dried ingredients, we create a crisp crust for these hens . . . you won't miss the skin at all. Skinless hens are not available in stores. You will need to remove the skin yourself. The thigh and leg will separate from the breast with the skin removed. Serve with steamed okra and field peas to complete the menu.
Serves 6

Four Cornish game hens after being split and skinned will produce about 3 lb. ready for use. Split the game hens and remove the backbone. Remove the skin. The breasts and leg quarter will separate. Preheat an oven to 350 degrees. In a bowl, combine the minced dried tomato, onion flakes, dried chives, dried garlic, celery flakes, and lemon zest. Combine into a pasty yet crumbly substance. Rub on the outsides of hens to create crust. Place on a sheet pan sprayed with vegetable cooking spray and roast for 25 minutes.

Duck and Sausage Cassoulet

Vegetable cooking spray
2 ducks, medium sized
2 tbsp. cracked black pepper
½ lb. turkey sausage, lean, sliced 2 inches thick
5 oz. tasso ham, spicy, sliced ½ inch thick
1 cup onions, chopped
½ cup carrot, chopped
½ cup celery, chopped
1 each fennel bulbs, cut into wedges
1 cup dry white wine
1½ quarts duck stock or chicken stock, or low-sodium broth
1 cup navy beans, dry
1 cup lima beans, dry
1 cup black-eyed peas, dry
2 bay leaves
1 cup fresh herbs, chopped
¼ cup balsamic vinegar
1 loaf French bread

Calories (kcal)	414
Total Fat (gm)	8
% Calories from Fat	18%
Cholesterol (mg)	50
Sodium (mg)	1085

Cassoulet is a dish that can take all day, if not two, to prepare. Here we have taken a few short cuts, but not so many that we steal flavor from the final product.
Serves 12

Preheat oven to 375 degrees. Cut the duck into pieces, removing the skin from the breast and thigh meat. Trim any excess fat. Pat dry with towels, then rub with pepper. Spray roasting pan with vegetable cooking spray, place duck pieces in pan, and roast in the oven for 25 minutes. Pick the meat from the bones. If time allows, prepare a duck stock with water from the roasted duck bones.

In the same roasting pan, sear the sausage and tasso ham, remove, and hold with duck meat. Add the onion and brown to a golden color, add the carrot, then the celery and fennel, allowing it to caramelize after each addition. Fold the navy beans, lima beans, and black-eyed peas with the caramelized vegetables. Add the white wine and cook for 2 minutes. Add the duck and the sausage, and the bay leaves, then cover with the duck or chicken stock. Cover and cook either on the stove or in the oven for 20 minutes. Fold in ½ cup of the fresh herbs. If it looks dry, add some water to finish cooking.

Cover and cook a further 30-45 minutes or until all of the beans are tender. Meanwhile, tear the bread into pieces, place on a sheet pan, and bake into crispy croutons. When the beans are tender and all of the rich flavors have married, add the balsamic vinegar and remaining herbs. Adjust the seasoning with salt and pepper. Serve the cassoulet in large bowls garnished with croutons.

Duck Breast with Grilled Radicchio and Sweet Bourbon Oranges

1 head radicchio, quartered
1 tbsp. extra virgin olive oil
Salt and pepper, to taste
4 oranges, skinned and sliced
½ cup sugar
¼ cup brown sugar
¼ cup water
¼ cup apple cider vinegar
2 tbsp. fennel seeds
2 tbsp. bourbon
6 6-oz. skinless duck breasts
1 tsp. sage, minced
Vegetable cooking spray
3 tbsp. chives, chopped

If boneless, skinless duck breasts are not available at your grocery, whole ducklings can usually be found in the freezer department. Defrost and bone ducks as you would a chicken. Save bones and leg quarters for stock or another occasion.
Serves 6

Brush the radicchio with oil and season with salt and pepper. Heat a grill and sear radicchio on each side. In a medium sauce pan, combine the sugar, brown sugar, water, vinegar, and fennel seed. Heat to a simmer and cook until sugar melts. Turn off fire from under sauce and add the bourbon. Remove the skins from oranges and slice into wheels. Place in a bowl and pour the hot syrup on top. Allow to cool. Heat a sauté pan with cooking spray. Season duck breasts with salt, pepper, and sage. Sear breast 2 minutes on each side, or until cooked through. Serve the duck over grilled radicchio and pour orange sauce and oranges over duck. Garnish with chives.

Calories (kcal)	*462*
Total Fat (gm)	*16*
% Calories from Fat	*31%*
Cholesterol (mg)	*175*
Sodium (mg)	*175*

Holiday Turkey with Peppered Dressing

6-8 lb. whole turkey
1 onion, coarsely chopped
2 stalks celery, coarsely chopped
1 bunch fresh thyme, coarsely chopped
2 lemons, quartered
2 tsp. kosher salt
2 tsp. cracked black pepper
1 tsp. fresh thyme, picked and chopped
½ tsp. baking powder
6 cups fresh bread crumbs, toasted
6 cups corn bread, crumbled and toasted
3 egg whites, lightly beaten
Vegetable cooking spray
1 onion, chopped
2 stalks celery, chopped
1½ cups chicken or turkey stock, defatted

The key to a great roast turkey is to not overcook it. A good trick is to use small birds. The breast meat will not dry out while waiting for thigh meat to finish cooking. If serving a large number of people, rather than purchase a large bird, buy two small ones. Remove skins to lower fat and calories. Garnishing with fresh thyme stalks and candied lemon peel makes a beautiful presentation.
Serves 12

Preheat an oven to 325 degrees. Rinse the turkey inside and out, removing the giblets and neck. Pat dry. Trim any excess fat and skin from around the neck and cavity. If a band of skin crosses the tail, tuck the drumsticks under the band. Otherwise truss the legs to the tail. Twist the wings tips under the back. Fill the cavity with onion, celery, thyme, and lemon. Place on a roasting rack in a large roasting pan. Roast for 2 hours. All ovens behave differently, so after 1½ hours check internal temperature. Place a thermometer into the thigh of the bird. Temperature should read 165 degrees.

Meanwhile, combine the salt, pepper blend, thyme, baking powder, bread crumbs, corn bread crumbs, and egg whites in a bowl. Spray a medium glass baking dish with vegetable cooking spray, and gently sauté the onion and celery over the stove, add the chicken or turkey stock, and bring to a simmer. Add the stuffing and fold until completely combined. Add more stock if you like a "wetter" dressing. Cover and place in the oven with the turkey and bake 45 minutes.

Remove turkey from oven, and allow to rest for at least 30 minutes. Discard the vegetables and lemons in the cavity. Serve the turkey with the stuffing.

Calories (kcal)	719
Total Fat (gm)	26
% Calories from Fat	33%
Cholesterol (mg)	195
Sodium (mg)	1626

Lime-Marinated Emu Fajitas with Pumpkin Seeds

1½ lb. boneless emu tenderloin, cut into strips
1 tbsp. lime juice
3 tbsp. thyme
1 tsp. ground cumin
½ tsp. nutmeg
2 tsp. salt
Vegetable cooking spray
1 cup red onion, sliced
2 tbsp. garlic, mashed
1 cup white wine
½ cup low-sodium beef broth
⅓ cup roasted pumpkin kernels, toasted
12 flour tortillas
3 limes, cut into wedges

The use of emu and ostrich is on the rise due to the full flavor in a very lean package. If they are not available, this recipe is very good with skinless chicken breasts or lean pork fillets. The fun of fajitas is in the sizzle. Anyone can prepare fajitas using these directions. Serve with rice, beans, and fresh tomatoes to complete the menu.
Serves 6

Preheat oven to 375 degrees. Place a clean fajita pan or cast-iron skillet in the oven and allow to heat. Combine the emu strips with 1 tbsp. of lime juice, thyme, cumin, nutmeg, and salt. On the stove, heat a separate skillet over medium heat. Spray with vegetable cooking spray, and sear the emu. Do not stir too much in the skillet. Rather, allow it to caramelize and sear it before agitating. Add the onions and garlic and cook further until caramelized. Add the wine. Cook 1 minute, then add the beef broth. Just before serving, remove cast-iron skillet or fajita pan from the oven. Add emu fajitas to hot pan. Sprinkle with pumpkin seeds, and serve with warm tortillas.

Calories (kcal)	453
Total Fat (gm)	12
% Calories from Fat	24%
Cholesterol (mg)	53
Sodium (mg)	1155

Pollo Spanish Rice

- 1 tbsp. chili powder
- ½ tsp. cumin, ground
- 1 tsp. orange zest
- 1 tsp. lime zest
- 1 lb. chicken breast halves without skin, diced
- 1 tbsp. corn oil
- ½ tbsp. garlic, minced
- ¾ cup onion, diced
- 1½ cups rice, instant
- ½ cup white corn kernels, frozen
- 1 tsp. salt
- 3 cups chicken stock, or low-sodium broth
- ½ cup Roma tomato, seeded and chopped
- 3 tbsp. chopped parsley

A good way to recognize less-saturated fats is the bottle test. If it pours it is probably a more unsaturated fat. Does that mean all oils are created equal? Many unsaturated fats are full of great flavor. To intensify flavor in a dish, pick the right flavor. Olive oil is used for Italian or French foods, but a little corn oil can accent Spanish or Mexican foods.
Serves 6

Combine the chili powder, cumin, orange zest, and lime zest in a bowl. Sprinkle over the chicken to season. Heat the corn oil in a sauce pan, and sauté the onion and garlic. Add the chicken and sauté until barely opaque, about 3 minutes. Add the rice and corn; sauté for about half a minute to combine. Add the chicken stock and salt, bring to a boil, reduce the heat to low, and cover. Cook for 20 minutes, or until rice is tender. Toss the tomatoes and parsley in the rice just before serving.

Calories (kcal)	221
Total Fat (gm)	4
% Calories from Fat	18%
Cholesterol (mg)	35
Sodium (mg)	874

Simple Szechuan Stir-Fry

- 3 lb. chicken breast halves without skin, sliced ½-inch thick
- 2 tbsp. peanut oil
- 1 tbsp. garlic, minced
- 1 tbsp. ginger root, minced

Serve with steamed rice and marinated cucumber salad.
Serves 8

Trim chicken of any fat, and slice against the grain. Heat a wok with peanut oil until "smoking" hot. Add the garlic, ginger, and chilies. Next, add the onion and bell pepper and stir-fry together for 1 minute. Add the chicken and stir-fry 3 minutes. Add the soy, broth, sugar, and pepper. Cook for 2 more

- 2 hot chili peppers, sliced
- 1 onion, sliced
- 1 red bell pepper, sliced
- 1 tbsp. low-sodium soy sauce
- ¼ cup low-sodium chicken broth
- ½ tsp. sugar
- ¼ tsp. cracked black pepper
- 1 tsp. cornstarch
- 2 tbsp. water

minutes. Dissolve the cornstarch in water, then add to stir-fry to thicken.

Calories (kcal)	202
Total Fat (gm)	5
% Calories from Fat	24%
Cholesterol (mg)	79
Sodium (mg)	182

Tandoori Chicken

- 2 lb. chicken breast halves without skin
- 1 tbsp. paprika
- 2 tsp. cumin seed
- 2 tsp. coriander seed
- 4 cloves garlic, mashed
- 2 tbsp. ginger root, minced
- 2 jalapeno peppers, minced
- ¾ cup plain non-fat yogurt
- 1 tsp. lime zest

Serve with basmati rice, cooked lentils, and a flavorful mango chutney to complete the menu.
Serves 8

Trim chicken breasts of any fat and remove the skin. Grind the cumin and coriander seeds fresh. Place paprika, cumin, and coriander in a small sauté pan and toast over a low flame until the aromas are released. Combine spices, garlic, ginger, peppers, yogurt, and zest. Mix well before adding chicken. Mix to coat. Marinate for at least 1 hour to overnight. Prepare a grill. Grill chicken slowly on medium heat with the lid down to accumulate the smoky flavor, about 25 minutes, depending on the size of the breasts. Do not overcook and dry out.

Calories (kcal)	125
Total Fat (gm)	2
% Calories from Fat	11%
Cholesterol (mg)	53
Sodium (mg)	78

CHAPTER 7

Fish and Seafood

*Barbecued Shrimp with
  Sweet Corn and Potatoes*
Crab Tamales with Ancho Chili Sauce
Crawfish Eggrolls
Crawfish Pappardelle with Tomato Brochette
Creole Crab Cakes with Roasted Garlic Sauce
*Drum Fish with Johnny Cakes
  and Creole Red Bell Sauce*
*Grilled Lobster and Asparagus with
  Chervil Butter*
New England Seafood Pie
Orange Shrimp and Fennel Kabobs
*Pan-Roasted Red Snapper with
  Sherry Turtle Sauce*
Pompano au Papier
Roasted Eggplant with Creole Crawfish
Salmon Niçoise
*Scallops in Champagne Sauce over
  Spring Vegetables*
Seafood Jambalaya

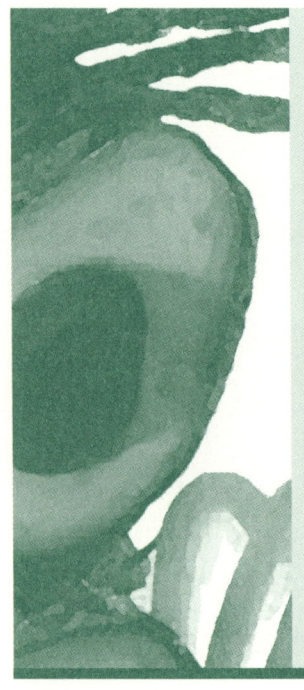

Seared Catfish with Creole Mustard Sauce
 and Dirty Rice
Sizzling Shrimp Fajitas with Confetti Peppers
Speckled Trout with Sazerac Sauce
Spiced Moroccan Shrimp over Couscous
Spring Trout with Lime Vinaigrette
Steamed Clams and Mussels with
 Tasso Cuisson
Steamed Clams with Cilantro and Lime
Swiss Chard Halibut with Ginger Sauce
Thai Steamed Mussels
Tuscan Seafood Bake

Barbecued Shrimp with Sweet Corn and Potatoes

4 ears sweet white corn, whole
4 tbsp. unsalted margarine, melted
²⁄₃ cup pickapeppa sauce
¹⁄₃ cup balsamic vinegar
4 tbsp. fresh rosemary, chopped
2 tbsp. fresh basil, chopped
1 tsp. dry oregano
1 lemon
Pinch cayenne, to taste
1 tsp. cracked black pepper
½ lb. small red potatoes, quartered
3 lb. shrimp, with shells and heads
Salt, to taste

Serve with a simple green tossed salad and crispy soft French bread to soup-up all of the good cooking juices. Pickapeppa sauce, found near the barbecue sauce and catsup in the grocery, is a wonderful rich pepper-mash sauce. If not available, substitute Worcestershire sauce.
Serves 6

Preheat an oven to 375 degrees. Wrap the ears of corn in aluminum foil . . . the whole thing! . . . husks, silk, and all. Place in oven for 1 hour. Remove from oven and let cool 5 minutes. Remove the foil. Pull the husk down and remove the silk.

Meanwhile, combine the melted butter, pickapeppa sauce, balsamic vinegar, rosemary, basil, oregano, lemon, cayenne, and black pepper in a bowl. Add the salt, according to taste. Toss 3 tbsp. of dressing with the potatoes. Lay potatoes flat on a sheet pan, and roast in the oven with the corn for 25 minutes or until golden and tender.

In a bowl, toss the shrimp in the remaining dressing and allow to marinate for 30 minutes. Pour shrimp and marinade into a shallow baking dish. Preheat a broiler and broil the shrimp for 5 minutes, toss and turn the shrimp, and broil another 5 minutes. Serve the shrimp in bowls with potatoes and roasted corn swimming in the cooking juices.

Calories (kcal)	411
Total Fat (gm)	12
% Calories from Fat	26%
Cholesterol (mg)	345
Sodium (mg)	726

Crab Tamales with Ancho Chili Sauce

12 each corn husks
1¾ cups Masa Harina, or corn meal
⅓ tsp. baking powder
½ tsp. salt
2 tsp. sugar
2½ tbsp. cilantro, chopped
⅓ cup Parmesan cheese, grated
1¼ cups creamed corn, fresh if possible
4 tbsp. shortening
½ cup skim milk
2 tsp. corn oil
1 tsp. garlic
2 tsp. roasted chili pods, chopped
2 tsp. chili powder
1½ cups white wine
1½ pints crab stock or shrimp stock
1½ lb. lump crab meat
⅓ cup colored bell peppers, brunoise, or diced
½ each jalapeno, minced
1 tsp. lemon juice

These tamales freeze! For an easy mid-week meal, just pull a few rolled tamales out of the freezer and let defrost. Then steam and prepare the sauce. It's simple. Serve two tamales as a portion, but one makes for an elegant appetizer.
Serves 6

Soak the dried corn husks in hot water for 30 minutes. Combine the masa, baking powder, salt, sugar, cilantro, Parmesan, and corn. Cut the butter into the masa mixture and blend like biscuit dough. Add the milk until there is a smooth, spreadable consistency. Spoon about 3 tbsp. of mixture into the center of husks, roll, and place seams down in a steamer. Steam for 15 minutes.

In a medium sauté pan, sauté garlic in corn oil. Add the chili pods and chili powder. Deglaze with white wine. Add the stock and bring to a simmer. Add the crab meat, bell peppers, and jalapeno. Season with lemon juice. To serve, split open the tamale while in the husks (like a baked potato) and spoon seafood mixture over and inside.

Calories (kcal)	450
Total Fat (gm)	15
% Calories from Fat	32%
Cholesterol (mg)	92
Sodium (mg)	1193

Crawfish Eggrolls

2 tbsp. tasso ham, finely chopped
1 cup onion, minced
1 tbsp. garlic, minced
Vegetable cooking spray
1 tbsp. flour
2 tbsp. parsley, chopped
1 lb. crawfish, chopped
Salt and pepper to taste
¼ cup scallions, thinly sliced
1 lemon
32 sheets filo dough
¼ cup hoisin sauce
2 tbsp. low-sodium chicken broth
2 tbsp. scallions, garnish

Serve with stir-fried vegetables and steamed rice for a meal or alone for a great hors d'oeuvre or side dish. Kids love finger foods, and this is sure to be a fun, healthy snack. Freeze eggrolls uncooked, but make sure to unwrap them while they defrost, or the pastry will tear. You may substitute lean chicken breast or lean ground pork for the crawfish. Just stay away from the fryer!
Serves 6

In a medium sauté pan, sauté the tasso, onion, and garlic with vegetable cooking spray on low heat for 2 minutes. Sprinkle flour over mixture and cook an additional 2 minutes. Fold the crawfish and scallions into mixture and season to your taste with salt, pepper, and lemon juice. Allow to cool slightly.

Preheat oven to 350 degrees. Lay a filo sheet laterally on a clean, dry working space. Spray with vegetable cooking spray. Add another sheet on top. Spray again. Repeat until there are 4 layers of sheets. Cut in half vertically. This will prepare 2 large eggrolls. Place ¼ cup of filling in the center of each eggroll. Roll up like a jelly roll. Fold end seams underneath and lay on a sheet pan. Repeat for the rest of the filling. Bake until golden brown, about 25 minutes. Mix the hoisin sauce and stock together, and serve on the side. Garnish with sliced scallions.

Calories (kcal)	412
Total Fat (gm)	9
% Calories from Fat	19%
Cholesterol (mg)	90
Sodium (mg)	721

Crawfish Pappardelle with Tomato Brochette

- 1 sourdough baguette bread, sliced ½-inch thick
- 2 cloves garlic, halved
- 1 cup Roma tomato, seeded and chopped
- 1 tbsp. Italian parsley, chopped
- 1 tsp. balsamic vinegar
- 1 tsp. extra virgin olive oil
- Cracked black pepper, to taste
- 10 oz. pappardelle pasta, or fettucine
- 1 tsp. olive oil
- ¾ cup onion, sliced
- 2 tbsp. garlic, chopped
- 1½ lb. crawfish
- 1 tbsp. tomato paste
- ½ cup red bell pepper, chopped
- ¼ cup green bell pepper, chopped
- 1 jalapeno, chopped
- ½ cup red wine
- 1 cup seafood stock, or chicken stock
- ½ cup Gorgonzola cheese
- ½ cup scallion, chopped

Pappardelle is a type of pasta that looks like long, thin, wide ribbons. At the same time, parparadele is used in a traditional pasta dish of chipped pork with tomato-style sauce—very rich indeed. Our version is lean, yet gets its richness from the crawfish. When serving pasta, cheese can really turn a healthy dish into one full of saturated fat. Gorgonzola is a fairly strong ripe cheese that many people are wary of using. The idea is that a little will go a long way to make sure that flavor permeates the entire dish. Give it a try. I think you will be pleasantly surprised. Substitute blue cheese, or even a hard cheese such as Asiago, Romano, or Parmesan for a milder flavor.
Serves 6

Cut the Italian bread into slices at a sharp angle to create long, thin spears. Bake in a 350-degree oven until toasted lightly. Rub the toasts with the halved garlic cloves. This will coat the toast with an invisible but delightful piercing garlic heat to complement the tomatoes. It is optional to chop the garlic and add to the tomato mixture. In a small bowl, combine the tomato, Italian parsley, balsamic vinegar, extra virgin olive oil, and cracked black pepper.

Bring a large pot of water to a boil, season with salt, and cook pasta until tender. Drain and hold to the side. In a large sauté pan, sauté the onion and garlic with olive oil for 2 minutes.. Add the crawfish, tomato paste, and peppers. Cook on medium heat until tomato begins to stick to pan and lightly caramelize. Add wine and cook 5 minutes. Add stock, and reduce for 3-5 minutes, then add cheese and combine until melted. Toss the crawfish sauce with pasta, adding scallions. Top bread toasts with tomato mixture and serve with pasta.

Calories (kcal)	569
Total Fat (gm)	9
% Calories from Fat	15%
Cholesterol (mg)	138
Sodium (mg)	898

Creole Crab Cakes with Roasted Garlic Sauce

1 clove garlic
3 tbsp. water
2 lb. lump crab meat
2 tbsp. red bell pepper, diced
2 tbsp. red onion, minced
2 tsp. jalapeno pepper, minced
1 tbsp. fresh lemon juice
1 cup bread crumbs
2 tbsp. unsalted butter, melted
4 egg whites, whipped lightly
Vegetable cooking spray
¾ cup fat-free mayonnaise
1 tsp. lemon juice
½ tsp. cracked black pepper

Serve as an appetizer or over fresh steamed spinach for a complete meal. The presentation of the crab cakes is even more beautiful when you use a little yellow or orange bell pepper for color, reserving some of the minced peppers to sprinkle as garnish before serving.
Serves 6

Cut the top off the whole head of garlic. Place in a baking container with 3 tbsp. of water, cover, and roast in a 350-degree oven for 40 minutes. Combine the crab meat, bell pepper, onion, jalapeno, lemon juice, bread crumbs, melted butter, and whipped egg whites. Shape into small cakes. Spray a sheet pan with cooking spray. Place crab cakes on sheet pan, then spray tops of uncooked crab cakes. Bake in 375-degree oven for 10 minutes, turn over, and continue cooking another 5 minutes.

Remove garlic from oven. Squeeze out the soft, roasted garlic pulp from the paper-like skin of the clove. Mix with mayonnaise, lemon juice, pepper, and enough water for a smooth consistency. Drizzle over cakes or serve on the side.

Calories (kcal)	278
Total Fat (gm)	7
% Calories from Fat	23%
Cholesterol (mg)	129
Sodium (mg)	857

Drum Fish with Johnny Cakes and Creole Red Bell Sauce

6 Roma tomatoes, sliced ½-inch thick
Salt and pepper, to taste
3 roasted red peppers
1½ tbsp. balsamic vinegar
¼ cup water
1 cup cornmeal
1 cup flour
2 tbsp. sugar
4 tsp. baking powder
2 eggs
½ cup skim milk
2 tbsp. corn oil
1 tbsp. jalapeno, minced
2½ lb. drum, freshwater, fillet
3 tbsp. fresh herbs, chopped
2 lemon wedges

This recipe is a meal in itself. No need to worry about side dishes. Probably a green salad is all you need. Drum fish can be replaced by any tender, white flesh fish such as speckled trout, lake bream, or even small, tender catfish fillets.
Serves 6

Place tomatoes on a sheet pan and season with salt and pepper. Broil the tomatoes for 8 minutes, or until cooked through and bubbly. Roast the 3 red bell peppers over a flame or under broil, then seal in an airtight container for 5 minutes. Remove seeds and skins of peppers, reserving as much of the cooking juices as possible. Puree the broiled tomatoes and roasted peppers with juices, balsamic vinegar, and water. Season with salt and pepper, to taste.

To make the Johnny Cake, combine the cornmeal, flour, baking powder, sugar, and jalapeno in a medium-sized mixing bowl. Form a well in the dry ingredients. Add the egg and milk in the well and mix together. Spray a medium sauté pan with cooking spray. Using a 2 oz. ladle or measuring cup, pour Johnny Cake batter into skillet as you would pancakes. Cook until bubbles form in the center of cakes, turn, and finish cooking on other side. Remove and hold on a platter.

Season fish with salt and pepper. Sear drum fish on each side until cooked through, about 5 minutes total. Place pan of seared fish fillets on Johnny Cakes to receive the juices. Lightly season the fish with lemon and drizzle Red Bell Sauce on top.

Calories (kcal)	*511*
Total Fat (gm)	*17*
% Calories from Fat	*29%*
Cholesterol (mg)	*182*
Sodium (mg)	*428*

Grilled Lobster and Asparagus with Chervil Butter

6 lobsters, 2 lb. each, live
2 lb. new potatoes
2 lb. asparagus
4 tbsp. unsalted butter
1 tbsp. garlic, minced
1 tsp. lemon zest
2 tbsp. chervil, chopped
½ tsp. salt
¼ tsp. cayenne pepper
1½ lemons, for garnish

Calories (kcal)	324
Total Fat (gm)	10
% Calories from Fat	27%
Cholesterol (mg)	164
Sodium (mg)	633

Flavor is intensified here by grilling the lobsters in their shells, thereby requiring very little butter. This is an elegant meal for special guests. Fire up the grill with your guests gathered around while sipping champagne. To complete the menu, serve a soup and salad to start, finishing with a Chocolate Raspberry Napoleon. If you are unable to find fresh chervil, tarragon is also very good to use.
Serves 6

Bring a large pot of water to a boil, add ½ cup salt and 8 bay leaves. Drop the lobsters into the boiling water. Cook for 8 minutes, drain, and cool on a rack or sheet pan. Meanwhile, boil the potatoes until they are tender. Drain, plunge into ice water, then drain again. Blanch the asparagus in boiling water, drain, plunge into ice water, and drain again. Whip the butter, garlic, lemon zest, chervil, salt, and cayenne together in a mixer. Finally, prepare a charcoal grill.

Pull the claws from the body joint, and crack a small hole in all three joints. Pull the head from the tails. The heads can be used for stock in another recipe. Uncurl and stretch the tail out on a cutting board. Split the tail with a long, sharp knife down the center of the tail. You now have one-half a tail, and one claw for each guest. When the grill is hot, rub a small amount of butter on the lobsters, potatoes, and asparagus. Place the potatoes flat side down, around the edges of the grill. Place the lobster tails face down on the hot grill so that the lobster meat is seared first. Cook for 3 minutes, turn, and cook another 2 minutes, depending on how hot the grill may be.

Try not to overcook; better undercooked than overcooked. Remove lobster from grill, turn potatoes, and replace lobsters with asparagus. Cook asparagus 3 minutes total. Remove all foods from the grill, melt the remaining chervil butter on top. Serve the grilled lobster, potatoes, asparagus, and lemon wedges on a large platter or divide among individual plates.

New England Seafood Pie

1½ cups onion, chopped
2 tbsp. garlic, minced
¾ cup celery, chopped
¾ cup green bell pepper, chopped
¾ cup red bell pepper, chopped
3 lb. shrimp, peeled and deveined
1 lb. bay scallops
1 lb. lobster meat
1 lb. lump crabmeat
1 cup white wine
1 cup parsley
½ cup basil
3 tbsp. chives
1 lemon, zested and juiced
1 tbsp. garlic, minced
1½ cups cream
12 sheets filo dough
Vegetable cooking spray

By preparing a filo dough crust rather than a traditional pie crust, we have reduced the calories and fat in this dish considerably. If one or two of the seafood items are not available, just omit and add more of another item. Complete this menu with a potato soup and green salad.
Serves 12

Spray a medium sauté pan with vegetable cooking spray. Sauté the onion and garlic for 1 minute. Add the celery, green bell pepper, and red bell pepper and continue cooking an additional minute. Add the shrimp, scallops, and lobster meat. Cook no more than 2 minutes. Seafood should still be slightly uncooked, but residual moisture removed. Remove from the pan into a large bowl. Add crab meat and allow mixture to cool.

Meanwhile, add the wine to the pan and reduce by half. Add parsley, basil, chives, lemon juice, zest, and minced garlic. Stir and then add the cream. Bring to a simmer, and cook on low heat for 5 minutes. Spray a 6-inch spring form pan with cooking spray. Lay one layer of filo dough into pan, allowing edges to fall over edges of the pan. Spray again and lay another sheet on top of the other. Continue the process to finish the crust. Fill crust with seafood filling, draining off any excess moisture. Bake in a 350-degree oven for 25 minutes. Serve with herb cream sauce.

Calories (kcal)	*348*
Total Fat (gm)	*11*
% Calories from Fat	*30%*
Cholesterol (mg)	*277*
Sodium (mg)	*579*

Fish and Seafood

Orange Shrimp and Fennel Kabobs

5 oranges
1 fennel bulb
2 tbsp. fennel, weed
3 lb. jumbo bay shrimp, peeled and deveined
3 tbsp. extra virgin olive oil
Salt and pepper, to taste

Fennel weed is the green frilly top of the fennel bulb, resembling dill. These kabobs produce a wonderful sweet flavor by balancing the sweet green anise flavor with the sweet anise bulb. Serve over rice or with creamy polenta (see page 156).
Serves 8

Cut 3 of the oranges into slices. Squeeze the remaining orange into a bowl. Cut the fennel bulb into thin wedges. Toss the shrimp in the bowl with the orange juice, fennel weed, and olive oil, and salt and pepper.

Prepare an outdoor grill. Skewer the shrimp with fennel bulb and orange slices. Grill for 3-5 minutes or until shrimp are just cooked through.

Calories (kcal)	267
Total Fat (gm)	8
% Calories from Fat	28%
Cholesterol (mg)	259
Sodium (mg)	270

Pan-Roasted Red Snapper with Sherry Turtle Sauce

½ cup flour
3 tbsp. vegetable oil
½ cup onion, minced
2 tbsp. garlic, minced
3 tbsp. green bell pepper, brunoise
3 tbsp. red bell pepper, brunoise
2 cups beef stock, or broth
1 cup turtle meat, chopped fine
2 oz. dry sherry
24 oz. red snapper, 6-oz. fillets
Salt and pepper, to taste
3 lemons, wedges
6 cups parsley, picked
2 tsp. garlic, chopped
2 tsp. lemon juice

We have lowered the fat tremendously by using a "dry" roux. By browning the flour, you achieve the chestnut color and aroma, but without the fat. Turtle soup lightly laced with sherry is a traditional soup in France as well as Louisiana. In this recipe, we have made a sauce rather than a soup, but with all the beautiful qualities of the soup. You can find frozen turtle meat in the freezer section of seafood markets. If not available, substitute crawfish, or omit the meat completely. The parsley salad will give this dish even further personality.
Serves 6

Brown the flour in a dry sauté pan, stirring constantly until very dark in color, but not burned. Remove from the pan and reserve. Heat 2 tbsp. of vegetable oil. Sauté the onion and garlic and slowly cook until brown and caramelized. Add the turtle meat and bell pepper; sauté 1 minute. Sprinkle with browned flour and blend thoroughly. Add the stock, stirring constantly, and allow to come to a simmer. Simmer for 15 minutes, skimming the top of sauce occasionally.

Meanwhile, heat a sauté pan with remaining oil. Season the fish with salt and pepper. Sear the fillets on both sides. Remove and season with lemon. Wipe out the pan. Add the garlic, parsley, salt, pepper, and lemon juice to the hot pan. Toss the sizzling parsley until barely wilted and crisp. Serve the fish over parsley salad topped with sauce.

Calories (kcal)	440
Total Fat (gm)	12
% Calories from Fat	22%
Cholesterol (mg)	42
Sodium (mg)	782

Pompano au Papier

6 pieces parchment paper, or baking paper
2 lb. pampano fillets
1 cup red onion, sliced
2 tomatoes, sliced
Salt and pepper, to taste
1 tbsp. sage, picked clean
1 tbsp. thyme, picked clean
1 tbsp. rosemary, picked clean
3 oranges
1 grapefruit
3 lemons
3 limes
2 tbsp. honey
1 tbsp. shallots, minced
2 tsp. garlic, minced
3 tbsp. parsley, chopped
4 tbsp. cold butter, cubed
¼ cup chives, match sticks

This is a traditional New Orleans dish. By baking in the oven with no pans, there is little cleanup afterward. This recipe is unique with its citrus beurre blanc. Serve with a small side of boiled new potatoes and a fresh green vegetable such as broccoli or green beans.
Serves 6

Season pompano with salt and pepper. Lay a large piece of parchment paper on a surface. Place 1 fillet on half of paper. Place some onion and tomato on top, with 2 sage leaves, a sprig of thyme, and 2 tbsp. of rosemary leaves. Fold parchment over, and fold edges of paper together to seal into a pouch. Repeat the process for remaining pompano fillets. Bake in a 375-degree oven for 25 minutes, or until cooked through.

Meanwhile, grate 1 tbsp. of zest from each of the 4 citrus fruits. Juice the grapefruit, oranges, lemons, and limes. Discard seeds. Combine the juice, zest, 2 tsp. garlic, shallots, and honey in a sauce pan. Bring to a simmer. Reduce heat and slowly whisk in the cold butter. To serve, cut paper pouches and pour sauce on fillets. Garnish with citrus wedges and chives.

Calories (kcal)	302
Total Fat (gm)	10
% Calories from Fat	25%
Cholesterol (mg)	86
Sodium (mg)	176

Roasted Eggplant with Creole Crawfish

Vegetable cooking spray
2 eggplants, sliced 1 inch thick
Salt and pepper, to taste
1½ tbsp. corn oil
2 tbsp. flour
2 tsp. garlic, chopped
½ cup onion, chopped
½ cup red bell pepper, chopped
1½ lb. crawfish tails
¾ cup white wine
½ cup seafood stock, or water
1 tbsp. basil
½ lemon

Serve with a green salad and toasted French bread. Another option is to replace the eggplant with portabella mushrooms. Cook the mushrooms in the oven as you do the eggplant and serve crawfish sauce on top.
Serves 6

Preheat an oven to 400 degrees. Spray a sheet pan with vegetable cooking spray. Lay the eggplant slices on the sheet pan and lightly sprinkle with salt and pepper. Roast in the oven for 20 minutes.

Meanwhile, heat a sauté pan with corn oil. Cook the flour in oil until chestnut in color, about 8 minutes on medium low heat. Add the onion and garlic until brown, sweet, and caramelized. Add the red bell pepper and crawfish tails with their juices. Sauté 2 minutes, then deglaze with white wine. Cook for 3-5 minutes, or until the "winey" flavor has cooked away. Add the stock, and season with basil and lemon. Reduce to your desired consistency, about 5 minutes. To serve, lay roasted eggplant on bottom of serving dish or individual plates and spoon crawfish over.

Calories (kcal)	189
Total Fat (gm)	5
% Calories from Fat	25%
Cholesterol (mg)	130
Sodium (mg)	122

Salmon Niçoise

- 1 can artichoke hearts, quartered
- 4 red potatoes, wedged
- ½ red onion, wedged
- ¾ cup green beans, steamed
- 30 oz. salmon fillets, skinned
- ½ tsp. kosher salt
- 1 tsp. cracked black pepper
- ½ tbsp. olive oil
- ⅓ cup Niçoise olives, pitted
- 1 tbsp. garlic, minced
- 1 bay leaf
- 1 sprig rosemary
- 1 cup water
- 1 cup dry white wine
- ½ cup Saffron Aoili, recipe found in book, optional

Niçoise olives are small, cured black olives from France. If they are not available, use any Greek-cured olive instead. Olive oil is a wonderful, full-flavored unsaturated fat, but be careful of the amount used. A good trick is to add olive oil to a hot pan and move around to the edges. If the oil "pools" near the edges, blot some out with a paper towel.

Serves 6

Drain and rinse artichokes and cut into bite-size wedges. Cut potatoes into bite-size wedges. Cut red onion into wedges, keeping the core in tact. Steam the green beans until tender, drain, and plunge in ice water. Season salmon fillets with salt and pepper. Heat olive oil in a sauté pan until very hot. Place salmon fillets presentation side down in hot pan. Allow to cook undisturbed until the edges are cooked and appear to be browning. Turn fillets and allow to cook on other side briefly. The center should still be rare to medium rare inside.

Remove from pan and keep warm. Blot remaining fat in pan with a paper towel. Add the artichokes, olives, potatoes, garlic, red onion, bay, and rosemary. Heat through before adding the water. Add water, cover, and cook 5 minutes or until potatoes are tender. Remove cover and add white wine, reduce by half. Just before serving, remove the bay leaf and rosemary sprig and toss in the green beans. Place vegetables on the bottom of plates or platter and lay salmon on top. Also great with a drizzle of Saffron Aoili.

Calories (kcal)	307
Total Fat (gm)	10
% Calories from Fat	31%
Cholesterol (mg)	82
Sodium (mg)	584

Scallops in Champagne Sauce over Spring Vegetables

2 cups steamed spinach
32 sea scallops, remove foot
1 tbsp. olive oil
Salt and pepper
1 tbsp. shallots, minced
½ tbsp. garlic, minced
2 cups champagne
1 cup asparagus tips
½ cup baby carrots
½ cup cherry tomatoes, halved
1 tbsp. Gorgonzola cheese

What do you do with the leftover champagne in the bottle when it goes flat, or that bottle given to you last Christmas that was never used? Cook with it! Serve this with mashed potatoes or skillet-roasted potatoes for a complete meal. The red caramelization of the scallops is beautiful and delicious in this dish, but shrimp, or even a mild fish, is also nice.
Serves 6

Steam 4-5 cups of fresh spinach, or use frozen to obtain 2 cups. Heat a sauté pan with olive oil. Season scallops with salt and pepper. Sear scallops face down in pan until crispy and browned on the outside, but just barely cooked inside. Prepare a nest of spinach on a warm platter or plate. Remove from pan and place directly on top of spinach. Add the champagne, asparagus, and carrots to the pan. Reduce the champagne by half while cooking vegetables. Add the tomatoes. Remove the vegetables from pan onto platter. Melt cheese into sauce and drizzle over scallops and vegetables. If you don't have baby carrots, just cut them into sticks. A sweet white wine may substitute for the champagne.

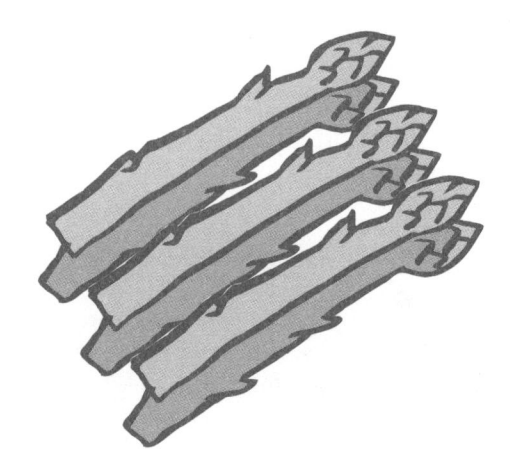

Calories (kcal)	161
Total Fat (gm)	4
% Calories from Fat	30%
Cholesterol (mg)	18
Sodium (mg)	279

Seafood Jambalaya

Vegetable cooking spray
6 oz. andouille sausage
8 oz. catfish fillets, seasoned
6 large shrimp, peeled and veined
1 cup yellow onion, chopped
2 tbsp. garlic, chopped
½ cup green bell pepper, chopped
1½ cups tomatoes, seeded and chopped
½ cup crawfish tails
1 bay leaf
2 tbsp. basil, chopped
Red pepper, to taste
3 cups converted rice
1 cup seafood stock
3 cups chicken stock
2 tbsp. parsley, chopped
6 crawfish, boiled

Seafood jambalaya is very similar to paella. Serve the jambalaya with a green salad and a plate of pickled vegetables, such as okra, green beans, corn, and olives. The tangy pickled flavor accents the starchiness of the jambalaya.
Serves 6

The cooking of the seafood is done in stages so as not to overcook and dry out the fish and shrimp. Spray a large cast-iron skillet with cooking spray. Sear the andouille until caramelized. Remove from the pan. Sear the catfish in the same seasoned skillet, remove, and hold. Add the shrimp, cook 2 minutes, and remove. Now, add the onion, bell pepper, and garlic to the skillet and brown until caramelized. Add the tomato, crawfish, bay leaf, basil, pepper, and rice. Combine until warmed through.

Add the stock, bring to a simmer, cover, and cook either in an oven or on the stove for 25 minutes. Uncover and add the parsley, shrimp, and andouille back to the pan. Do not stir the jambalaya too much or it will get sticky. Fluff with a fork for best results. Place the cooked catfish fillets and whole boiled crawfish on top of jambalaya to rewarm until service. To serve, dish out the seafood jambalaya mixture into bowls and garnish with catfish, shrimp, and whole crawfish.

Calories (kcal)	*593*
Total Fat (gm)	*15*
% Calories from Fat	*23%*
Cholesterol (mg)	*95*
Sodium (mg)	*909*

Seared Catfish with Creole Mustard Sauce and Dirty Rice

Vegetable cooking spray
½ cup ground beef, extra lean
½ cup onion, chopped
2 tbsp. garlic, minced
¼ cup green bell pepper, chopped
¼ cup celery, chopped
2 cups rice, washed
4 cups chicken stock, defatted
6 6-oz. catfish fillets, skinned
½ cup cornmeal
¼ tsp. cayenne pepper
1½ cups whole milk
3 tbsp. Creole mustard
3 lemons

Dirty rice is a dish served in Louisiana made with gizzards and liver. It is typically high in fat but rich in flavor. Here we "dirty up" the rice with leaner, healthier meats adding color, aroma, and flavor. Serve with steamed okra and corn bread to emphasize the soulful flavor in this dish—and maybe bread pudding for dessert!
Serves 6

Heat a medium sauté pan with vegetable cooking spray. Sauté the lean ground beef for 2 minutes. Add the onion, garlic, bell pepper, and celery. Sauté for 1 minute before adding the rice. Stir the rice to combine well, then add stock. Bring to a simmer, cover, and cook 20 minutes.

Heat a sauté pan with cooking spray. In a bowl, combine the cornmeal and cayenne. Coat fillets evenly with mixture. Sear the catfish on each side until cooked through. Remove from pan, and clean pan with a towel. Add milk and reduce it slightly. Fold mustard into sauce and season with lemon. Serve catfish over rice with sauce.

Calories (kcal)	*551*
Total Fat (gm)	*12*
% Calories from Fat	*19%*
Cholesterol (mg)	*114*
Sodium (mg)	*781*

Sizzling Shrimp Fajitas with Confetti Peppers

16 flour tortillas
2 lb. medium fresh shrimp, peeled and veined
2 tbsp. chili powder
2 tbsp. pickapeppa sauce
Cayenne, to taste
1 1/3 cups green bell peppers, seeded and julienne
1 1/3 cups red bell peppers, seeded and julienne
1 1/3 cups yellow bell peppers, seeded and julienne
2 tsp. jalapeno chile pepper, minced
1/4 cup red onion, sliced
1 tbsp. garlic, minced
2 tbsp. corn oil
3/4 cup beer
1/4 cup pumpkin seeds, roasted, optional
1/2 avocado, sliced

Serve these fajitas with Spanish rice and fresh chopped tomato salsa (pico de gallo). Steer away from garnishing your fajitas with sour cream or cheese. For a simple dessert, sprinkle flour tortillas with cinnamon sugar and bake in the oven until toasted. This is a great family meal that everyone will love. Substitute chicken for shrimp if you wish.
Serves 6

Preheat oven to 350 degrees. Place a clean cast-iron skillet or fajita skillet in the oven to heat. Place the tortillas in a warmer or wrap tightly in aluminum foil and warm in the oven. Combine the shrimp with the chili powder and pickapeppa; add the cayenne pepper, according to your taste. In another bowl, combine all the peppers, red onion, and garlic. Heat the corn oil on a griddle or in another large cast-iron skillet over medium-high heat. Add the shrimp to one side of the pan and the peppers to the other side. Allow peppers and shrimp to sear and become caramelized before tossing them in the pan. Eventually, toss the shrimp with the vegetables in the pan all together. Add half the beer to the skillet, and cook for 2 minutes. Toss the toasted pumpkin seeds and avocado with the shrimp.

To serve the fajitas sizzling, remove the hot skillet from the oven, transfer the shrimp fajitas into the new hot pan, and douse with the remaining beer. Now you can carry the sizzling fajitas to the table with a festive flare.

Calories (kcal)	576
Total Fat (gm)	17
% Calories from Fat	27%
Cholesterol (mg)	23
Sodium (mg)	1055

Speckled Trout with Sazerac Sauce

- 2 cups long-grain white rice, washed
- 2 tbsp. lemon juice
- ¾ cup basil leaves, chopped
- 2 lb. speckled trout, fillet
- 2 tsp. extra virgin olive oil
- Salt and pepper, to taste
- 4 oz. cognac
- 3 tbsp. sugar
- 1 cup beef stock, or low-sodium broth
- 2 tsp. bitters
- 2 tbsp. parsley
- 3 tbsp. butter

Sazerac is a famous and historic cocktail served in New Orleans. Here we have used the ingredients of the drink to prepare a refreshing sauce served over a mild white-fleshed fish fillet. I also use halibut or tilapia. Complete the menu by serving a salad, New Orleans-style French bread, and some fresh vegetables such as carrots, peas, or green beans on the side.
Serves 6

Cook rice in 4 cups of water. Fold basil and lemon into rice. Season trout fillets with salt and pepper. Heat a sauté pan with extra virgin olive oil. Sear the fillets with presentation side down. Reduce the heat, turn fish over, and cook until translucent throughout. Remove from the pan. Deglaze the pan with cognac. Be careful, as the pan might flame. Add the sugar and stock. Cook 3 minutes at a simmer. Add the butter gradually until emulsified, then add bitters. Serve fish over rice with sauce.

Calories (kcal)	*531*
Total Fat (gm)	*17*
% Calories from Fat	*32%*
Cholesterol (mg)	*103*
Sodium (mg)	*234*

Spiced Moroccan Shrimp over Couscous

2 quarts water
2 lb. shrimp
1½ tsp. ground ginger
1½ tsp. cinnamon
1½ tsp. cumin powder
2 tbsp. flour
2 tbsp. olive oil
2 cups onion, chopped
2 tbsp. garlic, chopped
3/4 cup raisins
2 lemons
2 tbsp. honey
2 cups couscous
½ cup cilantro, chopped
Salt and pepper, to taste

This is a great quick meal full of robust, wholesome flavor. Serve with slaw marinated in a vinaigrette, such as pickled slaw, and some toasted pita bread to complete the menu.
Serves 6

Remove heads from shrimp, peel and devein. Place shells and heads in a sauce pan on medium heat. Cook, stirring occasionally until shells begin to dry out and crackle (about 5 minutes). Add the water to pot, and bring to a simmer. Cook for 15 minutes, and strain stock from shells.

Meanwhile, in a large dry sauté pan, toast the ginger, cinnamon, cumin, and flour for 2 minutes on medium heat. Add the olive oil, onion, and garlic. Cook 1 minute before adding the shrimp. Thoroughly coat shrimp with the pasty seasonings, then blend in 2 cups of the shrimp stock. Bring to a simmer, add the raisins, juice of 2 lemons, and honey. Cook for 5 minutes. Cook the couscous with 3 cups of shrimp stock. Fold cilantro into couscous. Serve the shrimp over couscous.

Calories (kcal)	549
Total Fat (gm)	8
% Calories from Fat	13%
Cholesterol (mg)	230
Sodium (mg)	447

Spring Trout with Lime Vinaigrette

1 tbsp. canola oil
3 tbsp. lime juice
1 cup jicama, julienne
1 red bell pepper, julienne
½ cup leeks, julienne
½ jalapeno, minced
2 tbsp. cilantro
2 tsp. chili powder
2 limes, peeled and sectioned
6 rainbow trout fillets, whole, gutted
½ cup milk
1 cup flour, seasoned
Vegetable cooking spray
1 tbsp. shallot, chopped
1 tsp. garlic, chopped
1 tsp. sugar
½ cup lime juice
½ cup fish or chicken stock
Splash champagne vinegar
1 tsp. cracked black pepper
¼ cup chives, 1-inch sticks

If rainbow trout are not available, substitute any small river or lake fish such as bream or sacalait. Even though many people do not like fish served on the bone, you intensify the flavor by cooking a fish whole. Also, the perceived value of looking at the dish satisfies an appetite. Start your menu with a warm soup, such as potato and leek soup, then serve this recipe with Southern corn bread to complete the meal.
Serves 6

In a bowl, prepare the slaw by combining 1 tbsp. of canola oil, lime juice, jicama, bell pepper, leeks, jalapeno, cilantro, chili powder, and lime sections. Place in a cooler. Dredge the fish in milk, then flour. Shake off excess. Heat a sauté pan with cooking spray. Sear one side of fish crispy, turn, and place pan in 400-degree oven to finish. When all of the fish is cooked, remove fish from pan. Wipe out pan, and add the sugar, lime juice, fish stock, vinegar, and pepper. Whisk together away from the heat but in the hot pan until combined. To serve, place fish over a bed of slaw, pour vinaigrette over, and sprinkle chive sticks on top.

Calories (kcal)	359
Total Fat (gm)	11
% Calories from Fat	29%
Cholesterol (mg)	97
Sodium (mg)	137

Steamed Clams and Mussels with Tasso Cuisson

Vegetable cooking spray
2 oz. tasso ham, minced
2 tbsp. garlic, chopped
3 dozen clams, scrubbed
3 dozen mussels, scrubbed and bearded

Although eating mussels and clams can be messy, this is a great party dish. It is also a fun dish to introduce to your kids. Serve this recipe with a salad and assorted breads, or serve over a bed of angel hair pasta. Tasso is a lean, spicy smoked ham from Louisiana. If it is not available, use any lean smoked ham or an Italian ham such as pancetta or prosciutto.
Serves 6

Fish and Seafood

- 2 cups dry white wine
- 1 cup red onion, sliced thin
- ½ cup red bell pepper, julienne
- 1 tsp. jalapeno pepper, minced
- 2 tbsp. unsalted butter
- ½ tbsp. coarsely ground pepper
- ½ cup Italian parsley
- 6 slices French baguette slices, toasted

Heat a medium sauté pan with vegetable cooking spray. Add the tasso and garlic and sauté briefly, about 1 minute. Add the mussels and clams, stirring them to cover with garlic and tasso. Add the wine, and cover. Steam the clams and mussels until their shells open wide. Peek in the pot and remove them as they open. Arrange clams and mussels in serving bowls or on a platter. Add the onion, bell pepper, and jalapeno pepper to the cooking juice left in the pot. These juices are what is called a cuisson. Reduce for 2 minutes. Add the butter and pepper. Pour the hot steaming cuisson over the mussels and clams, and garnish with parsley. Serve with baguette slices to soak up the wonderful juices.

Calories (kcal)	*259*
Total Fat (gm)	*7*
% Calories from Fat	*31%*
Cholesterol (mg)	*39*
Sodium (mg)	*515*

Steamed Clams with Cilantro and Lime

- 4 dozen cherrystone clams, washed
- ¼ cup white onions, minced
- 1 tbsp. garlic, minced
- 2 cups dry white wine
- 1 cup cilantro leaves, whole
- ¼ cup lime juice
- 2 tbsp. unsalted butter

A wonderful dish as a starter for any tropical, Mexican, or Asian menu.
Serves 8

Place clams, onions, garlic, and wine in a large kettle. Bring wine to a boil. Reduce heat and cover. Steam clams until they open. Transfer clams to bowls. Transfer cooking juices to a food processor. Add cilantro, lime juice, and butter. Puree and then drizzle sauce over steamed clams.

Calories (kcal)	*127*
Total Fat (gm)	*4*
% Calories from Fat	*39%*
Cholesterol (mg)	*33*
Sodium (mg)	*44*

Swiss Chard Halibut with Ginger Sauce

4 lb. halibut fillets, thick cut
⅓ cup ginger root, minced
¼ cup shallots, minced
1½ tbsp. garlic, minced
1½ cups clam juice, bottled
1 cup dry white wine
1⅓ cups low-fat mayonnaise
16 leaves Swiss chard
1⅓ cups water
Salt and pepper, to taste

Use either red or green chard or even kale for this recipe. The flavor is delightful. Complete the meal with lemon rice and crusty French bread.
Serves 8

Season the halibut fillets with 1 tbsp. ginger, 1 tsp. shallot, and 1 tsp. garlic, salt, and pepper. Combine the remaining ginger root, shallots, garlic, clam juice, and wine in a sauce pan. Bring to a boil, reduce heat, and simmer 15 minutes. Remove from heat. Fold and whip with mayonnaise.

Meanwhile, wash Swiss chard and remove any thick stem or center vein. Place in a steamer and steam until just tender. Drain well. Wrap each halibut in a Swiss chard leaf, folding the ends underneath. Place fish pouches on a rack in a baking pan. Add 1 cup of water in bottom of the pan, cover with foil, and steam in the oven for 10 minutes. Serve with sauce.

Calories (kcal)	414
Total Fat (gm)	16
% Calories from Fat	38%
Cholesterol (mg)	86
Sodium (mg)	573

Thai Steamed Mussels

Vegetable cooking spray
2 cups red onion, thinly sliced
2 hot chili peppers, sliced
1 tbsp. ginger root, minced
½ tsp. coriander
½ tsp. turmeric

A beautiful, delicious dish. I usually prepare mussels very spicy, but you can regulate the heat content according to your liking. Although coriander and cilantro are the same thing, here I refer to coriander as the ground seed, while cilantro is the fresh grown leaves. This dish is also very good chilled.
Serves 6

Heat a large kettle with vegetable cooking spray. Sauté the onion, chilies, and ginger for 2 minutes. Add the coriander,

⅛ tsp. cinnamon
⅛ tsp. cardamom
¼ tsp. cayenne
⅓ cup coconut milk
2 tbsp. lemon juice
2 tbsp. cilantro, chopped
6 dozen mussels, whole

turmeric, cardamon, cayenne, coconut milk, lemon, and cilantro. Cook for 2 minutes, before adding the scrubbed mussels. Cover and steam for 10 minutes or until mussels have opened. Remove from kettle and serve immediately.

Calories (kcal)	227
Total Fat (gm)	8
% Calories from Fat	31%
Cholesterol (mg)	54
Sodium (mg)	555

Tuscan Seafood Bake

1 tbsp. extra virgin olive oil
1 cup onion, thin sliced
2 tsp. garlic, minced
3 sprigs sage
1 sprig rosemary
2 bay leaves
1½ cups rice wine vinegar
16 oz. salmon fillet
16 oz. amberjack fillet
8 oz. jumbo large shrimp
8 oz. sea scallops
½ cup capers or caper berries
5 sprigs Italian parsley, picked
½ oz. Parmesan cheese, grated
1 tbsp. cracked black pepper

This is a showstopper for a dinner party. For an easy, yet elaborate Tuscan party, serve with fresh tomato salad, small boiled red potatoes tossed in tarragon, steamed green beans, assorted olive tray, and assorted breads.
Serves 6

Preheat an oven to 350 degrees. Heat olive oil in a sauce pan, sauté onion and garlic, then add the sage, rosemary, bay leaves, and vinegar. Bring to a simmer. Place salmon, amberjack, shrimp, and scallops in an oven-safe baking dish. Pour hot marinade over seafood. Bake in oven for 20 minutes. Remove from oven and sprinkle capers, cheese, pepper, and parsley on top. If entertaining, prepare marinade, place seafood in a baking dish, and preheat oven ahead of time. After guests have arrived, pop everything into the oven. By the time everyone is seated, you are ready to serve it fresh and hot.

Calories (kcal)	288
Total Fat (gm)	8
% Calories from Fat	24%
Cholesterol (mg)	144
Sodium (mg)	470

CHAPTER 8

Meats of All Kinds

Beef and Portabella Mushroom Shish Kebab
Braised Pork with Sauerkraut and Apples
Cajun Meat Loaf with Smoky Tomato Sauce
Chili Roast with Glazed Tomatoes
Flank Steak with Olive Tapenade
Grilled Pork Chops with Calvados Apples
Grilled Veal Chops with Pear and Green Peppercorn Sauce
Grilled Venison with Roasted Onion Rings
Lamb Curry over Basmati Rice
Lamb Stew over White Polenta
Mambo Pork Loin and Island Fruits
Roast Veal over Creamy Polenta
Roasted Pork Loin with Herb Saint Green Sauce
Rosemary Grilled Leg of Lamb and Vegetables
Shepherd's Pie
Spiced Pork Stuffed Bananas
Veal Roulade with Caper Dressing
Venison Marsala with Rosemary Sweet Potatoes and Onions

Beef and Portabella Mushroom Shish Kebab

1 lb. beef sirloin steaks, trimmed of fat
2 cups red wine
1 tbsp. garlic, minced
2 tbsp. rosemary, chopped
½ tsp. salt
2 lb. portabella mushrooms, stemmed
1 pint cherry tomatoes
1 cup green onion tops, 1½ inches long
1 cup red bell pepper, 1-inch pieces
12 bamboo skewers (or rosemary twigs)

If you have a very healthy rosemary bush in your garden, cut long stems from the core of the plant and remove leaves. Use as the skewers for shish kebabs for flavor and appearance.
Serves 6

Cut the tenderloin into large 1½-inch cubes. Combine with the red wine, garlic, rosemary, and salt. Place in refrigerator and let marinate for 1 hour. Meanwhile, cut portabella mushrooms into 1½-inch cubes, wash tomatoes, cut green onion tops, and cut bell pepper pieces. If using rosemary skewers, pick hearty, long, woody stems. Pull rosemary leaves off stem, leaving 2 inches of leaf on top. Otherwise, soak bamboo skewers in water while meat marinates.

Remove meat from marinade. Place marinade on stove, and bring to a simmer. Skim top, and let cool. Skewer the meat, bell pepper, mushrooms, tomato, and green onion tops. Heat a charcoal grill or broiler. Baste skewers with marinade and grill skewers for 3-5 minutes.

Calories (kcal)	241
Total Fat (gm)	7
% Calories from Fat	32%
Cholesterol (mg)	24
Sodium (mg)	220

Braised Pork with Sauerkraut and Apples

1½ lb. pork tenderloin, trimmed
2 tsp. kosher salt
3 tbsp. poultry seasoning
1 tbsp. canola oil
1 cup onion, sliced
2 tsp. garlic, chopped
2½ cups sauerkraut, drained

Many people do not like sauerkraut because they have never had good 'kraut! Braising the pickled cabbage slowly in pork juices and apples is sure to be a hit. You'll love it. To complete the menu, serve with pumpernickel rolls, steamed potatoes tossed in dill, and a plate of soft cheeses, such as Brie or Camembert.
Serves 4

Preheat an oven to 350 degrees. Cut the tenderloin into 4 pieces. Roll the pork tenderloin pieces in poultry seasoning and sprinkle evenly with salt. Heat the canola oil in a medium Dutch

2 cups low-sodium chicken broth
½ Granny Smith apple, sliced
1 tsp. cracked black pepper

oven or baking dish. Pan sear the pork on all sides so the outside is brown and caramelized but still uncooked in the center. Remove from the pan. Add the onions and garlic to the pan, and sauté for 3 minutes. Add the sauerkraut, chicken stock, and sliced apple, and fold evenly. Place pork pieces in the mixture, cover, and cook in the oven for 45 minutes to an hour.

Calories (kcal)	*299*
Total Fat (gm)	*10*
% Calories from Fat	*28%*
Cholesterol (mg)	*111*
Sodium (mg)	*2408*

Cajun Meat Loaf with Smoky Tomato Sauce

Vegetable cooking spray
⅔ cup onion, chopped
1 tbsp. garlic, minced
⅓ cup carrot, chopped
⅓ cup celery, chopped
⅓ cup green bell pepper, chopped
⅓ cup red bell pepper, chopped
1 cup diced tomatoes, drained
½ cup bread crumbs
1 tbsp. Worcestershire sauce
Pinch cayenne pepper
Pepper, to taste
2 lb. ground pork, extra lean
2 egg whites
1 lb. lean ground beef
1½ tbsp. tasso, minced
1½ pints diced tomato, with juice
1 cup tomato sauce
⅓ cup green onion, sliced
Tabasco sauce, to taste

Ground pork may also be substituted for ground turkey. Serve with mashed potatoes and spinach salad for a great family meal.
Serves 6

Preheat an oven to 350 degrees. Heat a sauté pan with cooking spray under medium heat. Sauté the onion for 1 minute. Add the garlic, carrot, and celery, and sauté 1 minute. Add the red and green bell pepper and cook an additional minute. Transfer vegetables to a large bowl. Add the tomato, bread crumbs, Worcestershire, pepper, ground beef, ground pork, and egg whites. With clean hands, blend ingredients. Mold into a loaf and bake for 25-30 minutes. Meanwhile, combine the tomatoes, tomato sauce, and tasso in a small sauce pan. Bring to a simmer and cook for 15-20 minutes. Season with salt and pepper. Add the green onion and season with tabasco. Serve sauce with slices of meatloaf.

Calories (kcal)	*324*
Total Fat (gm)	*14*
% Calories from Fat	*38%*
Cholesterol (mg)	*121*
Sodium (mg)	*616*

Chili Roast with Glazed Tomatoes

1½ lb. beef tip round
3 tbsp. chili powder
½ tsp. cumin
1 tsp. black pepper
¼ tsp. red pepper
½ tsp. garlic powder
½ tsp. onion powder
2 lb. canned tomatoes, diced
3 tbsp. brown sugar, packed
¾ cup red wine
2 tbsp. chives, chopped
1 tbsp. parsley, chopped
4 cups cooked white rice, seasoned

Calories (kcal)	481
Total Fat (gm)	16
% Calories from Fat	31%
Cholesterol (mg)	71
Sodium (mg)	356

If you are unfamiliar with the term deglazing, this process is used after sautéing and roasting to create a flavorful sauce or gravy. When meats, seafood, or vegetables are sautéed or roasted, flavorful sediment stuck to the sides and bottom of the pan is left. The meat is removed, and wine, stock, or some sort of liquid is added to the hot pan to remove the flavors from the pan. This liquid is then reduced to develop color, flavor, and consistency.
Serves 6

Trim meat of any excess fat. In a bowl, combine the chili powder, cumin, black pepper, red pepper, garlic powder, and onion powder. Rub the roast in seasonings. Brown the roast with cooking spray in a Dutch oven or roasting pan. Place in the oven and continue cooking for 40 minutes, or until roast reaches desired doneness. Remove roast from pan and allow to rest for 20 minutes. Deglaze the pan with red wine. Add the tomatoes, brown sugar, and any remaining spices, and cook for 5-10 minutes on low heat. Fold chives and parsley into sauce. Slice roast and serve with rice and chili-glazed tomatoes.

Flank Steak with Olive Tapenade

2½ lb. flank steak, trimmed
1 tbsp. garlic, minced
2 tbsp. black pepper, coarsely ground
½ cup Worcestershire sauce

Flank steak is a great choice if you are craving the rich flavor of beef but want a lean meat for healthier living. Make sure not to overcook. Flank steak is best medium rare to rare because it depends on moisture for flavor and tenderness.
Serves 6

Trim the flank steak with garlic and pepper, add the Worcestershire sauce, and allow to marinate for half an hour.

¼ cup Greek olives, pitted and chopped
½ cup Italian parsley
1 tsp. garlic
2 tbsp. basil, chopped
2 tbsp. capers, rinsed
1 tbsp. Roma tomato, seeded and chopped
1 tsp. coarsely ground black pepper

In a food processor, or with a mortar and pestle, blend the olive, parsley, basil, garlic, and capers. Lightly fold the tomato and pepper with the tapenade. Heat a grill or large sauté pan and sear the steaks on each side. Spread the tapenade over a side, and slice thinly against the grain of the meat. Wonderful served with wild rice and steamed vegetables.

Calories (kcal)	380
Total Fat (gm)	21
% Calories from Fat	52%
Cholesterol (mg)	96
Sodium (mg)	542

Grilled Pork Chops with Calvados Apples

6 pork chops, thick cut
Salt and pepper, to taste
1 head cabbage, wedges
1 cup chicken stock
2 tbsp. fennel seeds
Vegetable cooking spray
3 Granny Smith apples, cored and wedges
1 tbsp. garlic, chopped
2 tbsp. brown sugar
2 oz. Calvados, or apple brandy
½ cup chicken stock
3 tbsp. chives, chopped

Calvados is an apple liqueur or brandy. By using liqueurs such as Calvados, we are able to increase the fabulous aromas of lower fat foods. This dish is lean only if you drastically trim the pork chops of fat. Substitute pork tenderloin if you wish.
Serves 6

Prepare an outdoor grill. Trim the pork chops of all fat and scrape the bone clean, leaving a 4 oz. piece of lean meat on a rib bone. Season with salt and pepper. Cut the cabbage into 6 large wedges, leaving the core in tact. Place in a baking dish, sprinkle with fennel seeds, and add chicken stock. Cover with top or aluminum foil, and bake in a 350-degree oven for 35 minutes. Meanwhile, sauté the apples in a pan with vegetable cooking spray. Add garlic and brown sugar. Turn off fire under sauce and add Calvados. Cook carefully, as the liquor may flame. Add chicken stock and cook for 5 minutes. Grill pork chops on grill for 3-5 minutes on each side or until cooked through. Serve over braised fennel cabbage and top with Calvados apples.

Calories (kcal)	344
Total Fat (gm)	16
% Calories from Fat	44%
Cholesterol (mg)	74
Sodium (mg)	279

Grilled Veal Chops with Pear and Green Peppercorn Sauce

5 lb. veal chops, with bone
Salt and pepper, to taste
1 tsp. vegetable cooking spray
1 pear, diced
¾ cup apple juice
½ tsp. cornstarch
2 tbsp. Calvados
1 tbsp. green peppercorns, in brine
1 beef bouillon cube
Vegetable cooking spray

Good quality veal chops make all the difference in this dish. Substitute the bouillon cube for a tablespoon of demiglace if available.
Serves 8

Prepare an outdoor grill. Season chops with salt and pepper. Meanwhile, heat a sauce pan with cooking spray. Brown diced pear, stirring sparingly. In a small cup, dissolve cornstarch in apple juice. Add to pear, with Calvados, peppercorns, bouillon cube, and thyme. Cook until slightly thickened.

Grill chops medium rare on the grill, about 10 minutes total. Serve with sauce.

Calories (kcal)	319
Total Fat (gm)	14
% Calories from Fat	42%
Cholesterol (mg)	161
Sodium (mg)	238

Grilled Venison with Roasted Onion Rings

2 lb. venison tenderloin, or back strap
2 tbsp. coarsely ground pepper
Pinch cayenne
½ cup balsamic vinegar
1 tbsp. garlic
1 onion, thinly sliced
Vegetable cooking spray

Venison has a wonderful, robust flavor. Those not accustomed to gamy flavors should try eating the back strap, which is much milder than a typical venison roast. If back strap is not available, use a venison roast, but cut roast into steaks and double the amount of marinade and marinating time.
Serves 6

Clean and trim back strap and allow to marinate in pepper and balsamic vinegar for 1 hour. Slice the onions paper thin. Preheat an oven to 375 degrees. In a bowl, toss the onions with olive oil and garlic. Layer onions on 2 sheet pans sprayed with cooking spray. Roast in the oven for 15 minutes. The onions will be dehydrated and caramelized. Remove from oven and allow to cool on pan. Prepare an outdoor grill.

Calories (kcal)	288
Total Fat (gm)	9
% Calories from Fat	29%
Cholesterol (mg)	124
Sodium (mg)	753

Grill back strap to medium rare on the grill, about 5-8 minutes. Slice thin against the grain and stack the onions on top.

Lamb Curry over Basmati Rice

3 tbsp. dark soy sauce
2 lb. lamb, cubed
½ cup onion, minced
1 tbsp. garlic, minced
1 tbsp. ginger root, minced
1 tbsp. curry powder
½ tbsp. paprika
½ tsp. coriander seed, ground
½ tsp. cumin, ground
1½ cups yogurt
3 tbsp. tomato paste
2 tbsp. dark brown sugar
2 cups basmati rice
4¼ cups water
½ cup peas
1 cup carrot, ribbons

This dish is a complete menu in itself. The colorful garnish makes the dish almost too pretty to eat . . . almost. Basmati rice is a long, thin white grain of rice found in Asian and especially Indian cuisine. It usually can be bought at the grocery, but if not available, substitute long grain rice washed of any residual starches.
Serves 6

Combine the lamb with soy sauce. Heat a medium sauce pan with vegetable cooking spray. Pan sear the lamb until golden brown, about 5 minutes. Remove lamb from pan, and add the onion, garlic, and ginger root. Sauté 1 minute. Add the curry powder, paprika, coriander, and cumin. Stir well and cook 2 minutes. Consistency should be "pasty." Re-add the lamb with the tomato paste, brown sugar, and yogurt. Cook until sauce comes to a simmer. Lower heat and allow to cook 10 minutes on low. Do not let sauce come to a boil or it will separate. Steam rice in water. Cook peas until just tender. With a vegetable peeler, peel carrots, then shave the peeled carrots into ribbons. Place in a bowl of ice water until ready to serve. To serve, pour curry over rice, garnish with peas. Drain carrots and prepare a nest of carrot on top.

Calories (kcal)	518
Total Fat (gm)	11
% Calories from Fat	19%
Cholesterol (mg)	106
Sodium (mg)	604

Lamb Stew over White Polenta

- 2 lb. lamb, cubed
- 2 tbsp. olive oil
- 2 tbsp. garlic, chopped
- 2 cups carrot, sliced
- 1½ cups frozen pearl onions, defrosted
- ¼ cup parsley, chopped
- 1 tbsp. Italian seasoning
- ½ tsp. salt
- ½ tsp. pepper
- 2 cups dry white wine
- 3 cups low-sodium chicken broth
- 2 bay leaves
- 4 cups mushrooms, sliced
- 2 tsp. cornstarch
- ½ cup water
- 1 recipe Creamy Polenta, see recipe
- ¼ cup caper berries
- 3 tbsp. Parmesan cheese, shaved

This wonderful lamb stew has been modified for a healthier diet, but still done in "Oso Buco Fashion." Serve with a chilled steamed asparagus and crusty sourdough bread to complete the menu.
Serves 8

Trim any fat from the lamb. Heat olive oil on a large Dutch oven. Add the lamb and garlic and cook 5 minutes. Add the carrot, pearl onions, parsley, Italian seasoning, salt, pepper, white wine, chicken broth, and bay leaves. Bring to a boil, reduce heat, and simmer uncovered for an hour. Add mushrooms and cook an additional 30 minutes. Prepare a slurry by dissolving the cornstarch into the water. Add to the stew. Cook an addition 5 minutes or until the stew thickens. Serve over polenta and garnish with caper berries and shaved Parmesan.

Calories (kcal)	366
Total Fat (gm)	11
% Calories from Fat	29%
Cholesterol (mg)	75
Sodium (mg)	505

Mambo Pork Loin and Island Fruits

- 2 lb. pork tenderloin, trimmed
- 1 cup orange juice
- ¼ tsp. allspice
- ½ tsp. cinnamon
- ½ tsp. cayenne pepper

Be careful not to overcook pork tenderloin. Because the tenderloin is so lean, it depends on moisture for flavor. The meat should still be light pink in the center. To complete this menu, serve mambo pork with black beans and crispy plantain chips.
Serves 6

Marinate the pork in orange juice, allspice, cinnamon, and

1 tsp. salt
1½ cups mango, pitted and chopped
1 cup papaya, seeded and chopped
¼ cup green onion, chopped
1 tsp. garlic
2 limes
1 tsp. olive oil
1 tsp. jalapeno, minced

cayenne for 1 to 2 hours. Remove from marinade, rub with salt, and roast in a 375-degree oven for 20 minutes. Meanwhile, combine the mango, papaya, green onion, garlic, jalapeno, juice from the limes, and oil. Warm slightly on the stove. Slice the roast and serve with the fruit salsa.

Calories (kcal)	242
Total Fat (gm)	6
% Calories from Fat	23%
Cholesterol (mg)	98
Sodium (mg)	434

Roast Veal with Pecan Orzo Pasta

2 lb. veal shoulder, trimmed and boned
1 tbsp. ground black pepper
Vegetable cooking spray
2½ cups orzo pasta
½ cup Boursin, or soft goat's cheese
½ cup pecan pieces, toasted
1 cup white wine
¼ cup onion
2 tbsp. garlic
3 tbsp. fresh thyme

Calories (kcal)	410
Total Fat (gm)	16
% Calories from Fat	37%
Cholesterol (mg)	105
Sodium (mg)	162

Roast veal is wonderful when cooked slightly medium-rare and served over a great side of orzo to catch all the delicious juices. Orzo pasta is small pasta in the shape of rice grains. You probably have eaten orzo in the popular product called Rice-a-roni and never knew it. Orzo cooks very quickly and easily, and you will find that your children will love it as well.
Serves 6

Preheat an oven to 375 degrees. Rub the roast with pepper and tie with string or butcher's twine. Heat on the stove a Dutch oven sprayed with vegetable cooking spray. Sear the roast on all sides until brown and caramelized. Place in the Dutch oven or a roasting pan, then roast in oven for 30 minutes.

Meanwhile, cook orzo pasta in a pot of boiling salted water until tender. Drain and toss in a bowl with Boursin and toasted pecans. Remove roast from oven, then remove from Dutch oven or pan. Blot any excess fat from the pan with a towel. Add the onion and garlic to pan and saute over medium heat. Add the white wine to deglaze the pan. Add the fresh thyme leaves to sauce. Slice the roast against the grain, ¼-inch thick. Serve over the pecan orzo with sauce to lightly glaze.

Roasted Pork Loin with Herb Saint Green Sauce

2 lb. pork tenderloin
3 tbsp. parsley, chopped
1 tsp. salt
2 cups white beans, soaked overnight
½ cup onion, chopped
5 cups chicken stock, or low-sodium broth
½ cup basil
¼ cup green onion, tops only
3 tbsp. extra virgin olive oil
2 tbsp. lemon juice
Salt and pepper, to taste
3 tbsp. Herb Saint liquor

Herb Saint is a liqueur with a sweet anise flavor. Paired with sharp green onion, the sauce should be drizzled or dotted over the meat as a hint of essence. You will love the sauce so much that you may want to make some extra to keep in the refrigerator for dipping breads. Enjoy!
Serves 6

Trim the loin of all fat, and roll in salt and parsley to coat evenly. In a small sauce pan, bring the onion, garlic, celery, beans, and stock to a simmer and cook beans until tender, about 1 hour. In a food processor, puree the basil, scallion tops, lemon, Herb Saint, and olive oil. Thin with stock if necessary. Season with salt and pepper. Heat a sauté pan, and sear the pork loin on all sides slowly until cooked through, about 5 minutes. Do not overcook. If the loin is very thick, finish the cooking in an oven at 350 degrees. To serve, slice the loin and serve over beans dotted with Herb Saint Sauce.

Calories (kcal)	540
Total Fat (gm)	14
% Calories from Fat	24%
Cholesterol (mg)	98
Sodium (mg)	1149

Rosemary Grilled Leg of Lamb and Vegetables

1 cup apple jelly
½ cup water
3 tbsp. rosemary
2 lb. tied leg of lamb roast, directions follow
20 twigs rosemary
Salt and pepper, to taste
2 tbsp. garlic, minced
1 cup pearl onions, blanched
1 eggplant, sliced
2 bunches asparagus, blanched
4 cups new potatoes, blanched
3 heads garlic, roasted

To prepare the tied leg of lamb roast, cut down along the line of the bone between the seams of meat. On the smaller end, cut closely around bone. Holding the bone upright, allow the meat to fall toward the cutting board. You will allow the weight of the meat to guide your knife around the final joint of the bone. Trim the meat of any excess fat. If it starts to fall apart, don't worry. You are going to tie the roast back together with butcher's twine. In this recipe you are not actually grilling the leg of lamb, but roasting it in a "rosemary oven." It's delicious. Serve with grilled eggplant, onions, potatoes, and roasted garlic.
Serves 6

Melt the apple jelly with the water in a small sauce pan and add the 3 tbsp. of rosemary. Remove from heat and allow to steep for an hour. Place rosemary twigs in cold water for an hour. Prepare an outdoor grill. De-bone and trim the leg of lamb. Lamb is a fatty meat. Only by boning and trimming severely can we lower the fat. Tie into a roast. Season roast with salt, pepper, and garlic. Sear the outside of the lamb roast on the grill. Place a nest of rosemary twigs on the grill, then transfer grilled lamb roast over twigs. Cover and cook until center is cooked through, but still medium rare. Remove from the grill and allow to rest for 30 minutes. Add the asparagus, onions, eggplant, and potatoes to grill. Lightly brown and caramelize with remaining coals. Remove. Serve sliced lamb with grilled vegetables.

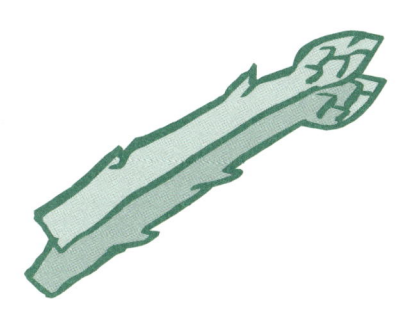

Calories (kcal)	*485*
Total Fat (gm)	*19*
% Calories from Fat	*33%*
Cholesterol (mg)	*81*
Sodium (mg)	*166*

Shepherd's Pie

Vegetable cooking spray
½ lb. lean ground beef
1 cup onion, chopped
1 tbsp. garlic, chopped
¾ cup carrot, large dice
1 cup mushrooms, sliced
1 cup canned diced tomatoes, drained
⅔ cup white wine
1 tsp. dried oregano
½ tsp. thyme
1 bay leaf
8 oz. frozen chopped spinach, defrosted
2 cups potatoes, peeled and cubed
½ cup skim milk

Great meal for the family on a Sunday night. May be frozen at the stage before baking for added convenience.
Serves 8

Heat a large sauce pan with cooking spray. Brown the meat until cooked through. Remove and drain. In the same pan, add the onion and garlic and sauté for 2 minutes. Add the carrot, mushrooms, oregano, thyme, and bay. Cook for 4 minutes before adding the tomato, wine, and cooked ground meat. Cook on medium heat for 20 minutes. Drain spinach well, pressing out any extra juices. Fold with meat.

Meanwhile, steam the potatoes in water until tender. Drain and allow to cool and air dry for 5 minutes. Place in a mixer with milk and whip until smooth. Season with salt and pepper. Preheat an oven to 350 degrees. To assemble, place meat and vegetables in the bottom of a rectangular Pyrex dish. Top with potatoes. Bake in the oven for 20 minutes or until warmed throughout.

Calories (kcal)	*175*
Total Fat (gm)	*6*
% Calories from Fat	*34%*
Cholesterol (mg)	*22*
Sodium (mg)	*63*

Spiced Pork Stuffed Bananas

Vegetable cooking spray
1 lb. lean ground pork
1½ cups onion, chopped
2 tsp. garlic, chopped
2 tbsp. curry powder
1 tbsp. tomato paste
½ cup low-sodium chicken broth
Salt and pepper, to taste
⅔ cup cilantro, coarsely chopped
8 bananas
½ cup fat-free sour cream
2 tbsp. lime juice

The true flavor of the pork comes not from the spices, but from baking in the banana skins. The sweet flavor permeates throughout.
Serves 8

Preheat an oven to 400 degrees. Heat a medium sauté pan with cooking spray. Sauté the ground pork for 3 minutes. Add the onion, garlic, and curry. Cook an additional 2 minutes or until the aroma of the curry rises. Add the tomato paste and broth. Stir over medium heat until the paste has blended. Season with salt and pepper and cook for 5 minutes. Turn off the heat and fold cilantro into filling.

Cut a slit lengthwise down each banana, and gently open the skins. Stuff each banana with spiced pork. Place in a roasting pan and bake for 25 minutes. Meanwhile, combine the sour cream and lime. Serve each stuffed banana drizzled with lime sauce.

Calories (kcal)	314
Total Fat (gm)	13
% Calories from Fat	35%
Cholesterol (mg)	55
Sodium (mg)	109

Veal Roulade with Caper Dressing

2 lb. veal cutlet, trimmed of fat
Salt and pepper, to taste
Vegetable cooking spray
½ cup onion, chopped
2 tbsp. garlic, chopped
¼ cup green bell pepper, chopped
¼ cup celery, chopped
2 cups bread crumbs
3 tbsp. Italian parsley, chopped
2 tbsp. capers, rinsed and drained
½ cup chicken stock, or low-sodium broth
1 bunch spinach, stems removed
½ cup flour, seasoned
2 tbsp. olive oil
1½ cups white wine
1 tbsp. capers
2 tbsp. parsley, coarsely chopped

Capers provide a delightful flavor similar to a cured green olive with delicate texture and packed with flavor. Capers, like pickles, are high in sodium, so be careful how much salt you use to season the veal.
Serves 6

Heat an oven to 375 degrees. Pound the veal cutlets thin. Place a piece of wax paper or baking paper on a clean surface. Piece the cutlets on the paper to make a large rectangle. Season with salt and pepper. In a sauté pan, sauté the onion, garlic, peppers, and celery with cooking spray. Remove to a bowl and combine with bread crumbs, parsley, capers, and stock. Layer the spinach leaves on top of the veal, then make a line of stuffing across the rectangle about half way. Roll the veal onto itself in jelly roll fashion. Tie with butcher's twine and sprinkle with seasoned flour. Set in the refrigerator for 20 minutes.

Heat a large sauté pan with olive oil on medium heat. Brown the roulade on all sides. Remove from the pan into a baking dish, and roast in oven for 25 minutes. Meanwhile, deglaze the sauté pan with white wine and reduce by half. Add the capers and parsley. To serve, slice the roulade and serve with the sauce.

Calories (kcal)	447
Total Fat (gm)	11
% Calories from Fat	25%
Cholesterol (mg)	127
Sodium (mg)	549

Venison Marsala with Rosemary Sweet Potatoes and Onions

- 2 tbsp. canola oil
- 2 lb. venison tenderloin
- 2 tbsp. fresh rosemary, chopped
- 3 tbsp. cracked black pepper
- 6 each sweet potatoes, peeled and cubed
- 2 cups pearl onion, skinned
- 2 sprigs rosemary
- 2 cups low-sodium beef broth
- ½ cup marsala wine
- 2 sprigs fresh rosemary

A venison tenderloin is also known as the back strap. Being very lean, the back strap is best cooked medium rare to medium in order for the meat to be tender and juicy.
Serves 6

Roll the tenderloin in rosemary and pepper. Heat a large sauté pan with canola oil on medium heat. You do not want your pan to get black specks from searing. Sear the tenderloin slowly on all sides until medium to medium rare inside, about 12-15 minutes. Remove from the pan and allow meat to rest in a warm place for at least 5 minutes. Add the sweet potato cubes and pearl onions to the pan. Sauté until brown, add 1 cup of beef broth, and steam until tender. Remove from the pan onto a platter or divide among plates. Add marsala to the juices in the pan and reduce by half. Place rosemary sprigs in sauce. Slice the tenderloin and serve over sweet potatoes and onions. Finish with marsala jus and garnish with rosemary sprigs.

Calories (kcal)	459
Total Fat (gm)	14
% Calories from Fat	28%
Cholesterol (mg)	124
Sodium (mg)	981

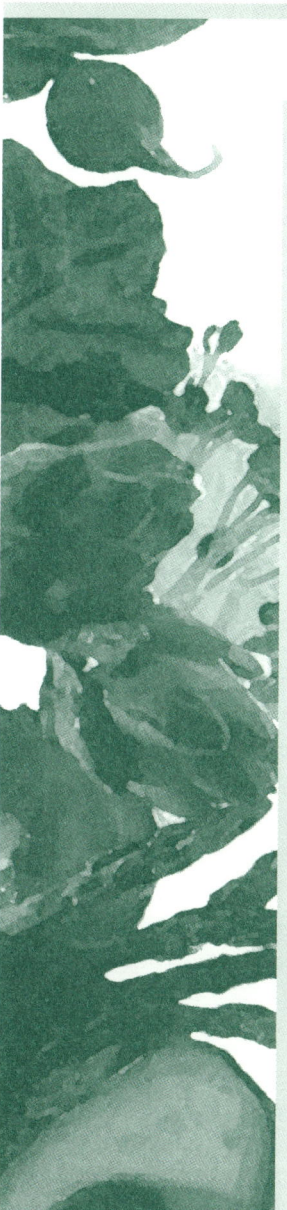

CHAPTER 9

Sauces, Dressings, and Garnishes

Artichoke Beurre Blanc
Balsamic Vinaigrette
Bourbon Sweet Onion Sauce
Brandied Peaches with Sun-Dried Cherries
Champagne Dijon Vinaigrette
Creole Mustard Dressing
Gingered Orange Cranberry Sauce
Herbed Ranch Dressing
Mint Chutney
Minted Far Eastern Marinade
Pickled Vegetables
Red Bell Tomato Sauce
Roasted Pepper Barbecue Sauce
Roasted Yellow Pepper Sauce
Saffron Aioli
Sun-Dried Tomato Pesto
Vegetable Marinara

Artichoke Beurre Blanc

3 artichokes, large, clean, cut in wedges
1 tsp. extra virgin olive oil
2 tbsp. shallots, minced
1 tbsp. garlic, minced
1 cup white wine
½ cup vegetable stock
3 lemons
3 tbsp. Italian parsley, coarse chopped
Salt and pepper, to taste
3 tbsp. butter, chilled, cubed

Calories (kcal)	151
Total Fat (gm)	7
% Calories from Fat	42%
Cholesterol (mg)	16
Sodium (mg)	277

Artichokes have a wonderful light anise flavor that pairs beautifully with so many foods. Toss this sauce with fresh arugula or spinach, serve with grilled salmon or any other light flaky fish, fold with sautéed shrimp over chicken breasts with steamed asparagus and green beans. The options are endless. The idea behind this recipe comes from a beurre blanc sauce. It is very high in saturated fat, but here a little goes a long way, with all the great flavor included.
Serves 6

Squeeze 2 lemons into a bowl of cold water. As you clean the artichokes, periodically dunk them into the lemon water to keep from browning. Remove leaves from artichokes, "snapping" at the ends to save the heart. Trim the stems and heart. Split artichoke down the center and top off. Remove the choke. Cut the artichoke hearts into 8 wedges.

Heat a medium sauté pan with one tsp. of extra virgin olive oil. Sauté the shallots and garlic, adding the artichoke wedges, and sauté until lightly browned. Deglaze with white wine and cook 2 minutes. Add the vegetable stock, cover, and steam for 5 minutes (or until hearts are just tender). Remove artichokes from the pan and gradually melt the chilled cubed butter into the wine sauce. Add the artichokes back to the pan, add the parsley, and adjust seasoning with salt, pepper, and lemon juice.

Balsamic Vinaigrette

1 tbsp. shallots, minced
1 tbsp. garlic, minced
3 tbsp. fresh herbs, chopped
1 sprig rosemary

This is a simple vinaigrette to drizzle on meats, toss salads, or dip bread. The percentage of fat is high in vinaigrettes because the nutritional value of all the other ingredients is so low (even the calories). But the flavors are all fresh and natural, so use this as a dressing or condiment with any of your favorite foods.
Serves 12

Sauces, Dressings, and Garnishes

½ tsp. salt
½ tsp. lemon zest
Pinch sugar
1 tsp. black pepper, cracked
⅓ cup balsamic vinegar
¼ cup extra virgin olive oil
2 tbsp. Dijon mustard

Combine all ingredients in a corked bottle or Mason jar. Shake and let sit at least 20 minutes before serving. Adjust seasoning with salt and pepper before service, if necessary.

Calories (kcal)	46
Total Fat (gm)	5
% Calories from Fat	87%
Cholesterol (mg)	0
Sodium (mg)	122

Bourbon Sweet Onion Sauce

½ tbsp. canola oil
1 quart yellow onion, minced
2 tbsp. garlic, minced
1 cup vegetable or beef stock
1 oz. bourbon
Salt and pepper, to taste

A great cooking lesson is to learn the difference between sweating vegetables and caramelizing vegetables. To sweat vegetables, we lower the heat and stir often. Here we want a rich golden brown color, so turn up the heat and rarely stir. The flavor is priceless. Serve with roasted pork loin, grilled chicken, grilled lean steak, rice, or potatoes.
Serves 12

Heat a medium sauté pan with canola oil, and caramelize the onion and garlic until golden in color. Add the stock and cook for 5 minutes. Add the bourbon and cook another 3 minutes. Then adjust the seasoning with salt and pepper.

Calories (kcal)	45
Total Fat (gm)	1
% Calories from Fat	22%
Cholesterol (mg)	0
Sodium (mg)	139

Brandied Peaches with Sun-Dried Cherries

2 lb. peaches, peeled
1½ cups brandy
1½ cups sugar
1 cinnamon sticks
2 star anise
½ tsp. whole cloves
½ cup sun-dried cherries

Calories (kcal)	214
Total Fat (gm)	0.3
% Calories from Fat	2%
Cholesterol (mg)	0
Sodium (mg)	2

Wonderful with rich meats or savory poultry dishes. Also a great Christmas present for friends and family.
Serves 12

To peel the peaches, bring a large pot of water to a boil. Plunge peaches into boiling water, and count to five! Remove to a bucket of ice water. Drain. Peel the skins from the peaches, halve, remove the pit, and place into large, hot, sterilized jars with the cinnamon stick, cloves, star anise, and sun-dried cherries. In a large sauce pan, combine the brandy and sugar. Place over medium heat and stir until sugar dissolves. Be careful because the brandy may flame over a gas stove. Pour over peaches up to ½ inch from the top. Allow to cool, and cover with jar lids. Store in refrigerator.

Champagne Dijon Vinaigrette

1 tsp. thyme, picked
2 tbsp. lemon juice
1 tsp. lemon zest
1 tbsp. black pepper, cracked
3 tbsp. Dijon mustard
½ cup vegetable stock
½ cup champagne wine vinegar
¼ cup canola oil
Pinch salt

Make a good portion of this to keep around for each and every day. Wonderful on all green salads. Place in a Mason jar and store in the refrigerator.
Serves 12

Combine thyme, lemon juice, zest, pepper, Dijon, stock, and vinegar in a bowl. Whisk oil in a fine ribbon gradually into dressing until fully emulsified. Season with a pinch of salt.

Calories (kcal)	54
Total Fat (gm)	5
% Calories from Fat	78%
Cholesterol (mg)	0
Sodium (mg)	116

Sauces, Dressings, and Garnishes

Creole Mustard Dressing

½ cup Creole mustard
½ cup vegetable stock
½ cup apple cider vinegar
½ cup canola oil
2 tsp. lemon juice
1 tsp. honey
Pinch salt

Serve with a spinach salad or any mildly bitter greens. A great appetizer is to drizzle over chilled, poached fresh fish, or toss with sautéed shrimp.
Serves 12

Combine all ingredients in a jar. Either whisk together or shake the jar just before serving.

Calories (kcal)	25
Total Fat (gm)	1
% Calories from Fat	21%
Cholesterol (mg)	0
Sodium (mg)	278

Gingered Orange Cranberry Sauce

2 tsp. canola oil
2 tbsp. ginger root, chopped
1 cup sun-dried cranberries
½ cup amaretto
1½ cups orange marmalade
½ cup slivered almonds, toasted

When cranberries are out of season, this recipe can come to the rescue. It is a wonderful relish for roast turkey, chicken, duck, or game hens. It is also beautiful spooned over Brie for an elegant hors d'oeuvre.
Serves 12

Sauté the ginger root in canola oil for 1 minute on medium heat. Add the sun-dried cranberries and fold together. Add the amaretto and cook for 3 minutes. Be careful to keep the alcohol from catching fire on an open flame. Add the orange marmalade, fold together, and remove from heat. Fold in toasted almonds. Great served over cheese or with roast turkey.

Calories (kcal)	205
Total Fat (gm)	4
% Calories from Fat	18%
Cholesterol (mg)	0
Sodium (mg)	25

Herbed Ranch Dressing

1 tbsp. cider vinegar
½ cup fat-free mayonnaise
½ cup fat-free sour cream
¾ cup buttermilk
1 tbsp. garlic, minced
½ cup fresh chives, chopped
¼ cup fresh parsley, chopped
1 tbsp. fresh tarragon, chopped
1 tbsp. fresh basil, chopped
2 tbsp. capers
Salt and pepper, to taste

Using fresh herbs for this delicious dressing makes all the difference. As an option, you may want to puree in a food processor for a colorful Green Goddess-style dressing. Use as a salad dressing, a dip, or drizzle over baked potatoes.
Serves 6

Beat together vinegar, mayonnaise, sour cream, and half of buttermilk. Stir in garlic, herbs, capers, and remaining buttermilk. Season with salt and pepper, if desired.

Calories (kcal)	51
Total Fat (gm)	0
% Calories from Fat	7%
Cholesterol (mg)	4
Sodium (mg)	253

Mint Chutney

3 jalapenos, minced
1 tbsp. fennel, ground
1 tsp. cumin, ground
1 tsp. coriander, ground
⅓ cup unsweetened coconut meat, shredded
3 cups fresh mint
½ cup cilantro leaves, whole

Serve as a marinade for chicken or pork for grilling, or as a condiment for any Asian, Far Eastern, or tropical menu.
Serves 12

Combine all ingredients in a blender. Puree until smooth in texture. Chill in a refrigerator for at least 2 hours before serving.

Sauces, Dressings, and Garnishes

¾ cup non-fat plain yogurt
¼ cup toasted almonds
2 tbsp. white wine vinegar
¼ cup lime juice
2 tbsp. honey
2 tbsp. grape seed oil

Calories (kcal)	*116*
Total Fat (gm)	*8*
% Calories from Fat	*59%*
Cholesterol (mg)	*0*
Sodium (mg)	*22*

Minted Far Eastern Marinade

1 cup yogurt
2 lemons
1 cup fresh mint, chopped
3 tbsp. garlic, minced
1 tsp. salt
½ tsp. cinnamon
½ tsp. red pepper
¼ tsp. allspice

Great with lamb or chicken. Marinate and grill meats, and use any leftover marinade for a sauce.
Serves 8

Place yogurt in a small bowl. Zest the lemon and juice. Add the lemon juice, zest, mint, garlic, salt, cinnamon, pepper, and allspice. Mix well and refrigerate until ready to use.

Calories (kcal)	*33*
Total Fat (gm)	*1*
% Calories from Fat	*25%*
Cholesterol (mg)	*4*
Sodium (mg)	*284*

Pickled Vegetables

¾ lb. red pearl onions
1 lb. baby carrots
2 fennel bulbs
1½ cups white wine vinegar
2½ cups water
⅔ cup sugar
2 tsp. salt

Serve pickled vegetables with sandwiches, on a relish tray as an appetizer, or give as gifts.
Serves 12

Peel red pearl onions. Peel and trim carrots. Cut fennel into wedges and remove core. Arrange the vegetables in sterilized jars. In a pan, bring the vinegar, water, dill, and salt to a boil. Pour hot liquid over the vegetables. Cool completely and cover.

Calories (kcal)	74
Total Fat (gm)	0.3
% Calories from Fat	3%
Cholesterol (mg)	0
Sodium (mg)	391

Red Bell Tomato Sauce

½ tbsp. extra virgin olive oil
1 cup onion, chopped
2 tbsp. garlic, chopped
1 cup red bell pepper, minced
3 cups tomato sauce
½ cup red wine
3 tbsp. balsamic vinegar
3 tbsp. fresh basil, chopped
1 tbsp. fresh chives, chopped
½ tsp. oregano, dried
Salt and pepper, to taste

The sweet flavor of red bell pepper and balsamic vinegar balance this tomato sauce for incredible flavor. Another great option is to use roasted garlic for even richer flavor.
Serves 12

In a medium sauce pan, heat the olive oil. Sauté the onion and garlic until caramelized, then add the red bell pepper and cook another 2 minutes. Add the tomatoes and cook 3 minutes. Deglaze with red wine and balsamic vinegar. Cook sauce for 15 minutes. Add the basil, chives, and oregano. Season with salt and pepper and serve.

Calories (kcal)	38
Total Fat (gm)	1
% Calories from Fat	17%
Cholesterol (mg)	0
Sodium (mg)	421

Roasted Pepper Barbecue Sauce

Vegetable cooking spray
½ cup onion, chopped
2 tbsp. garlic, chopped
1 tbsp. paprika
2 roasted red peppers, chopped
1½ cups crushed tomatoes, canned
½ cup brown sugar, packed
¼ cup balsamic vinegar
½ cup green onion, thinly sliced
Salt and pepper, to taste

To roast the bell peppers, place over an open flame on the stove or under broiler. Allow the skins to blister and char on all sides, then place in an airtight container to sweat for 5 minutes. The skins will slip right off. If you are short of time and energy, roasted bell peppers can now be found in jars at the grocery, or you may substitute pimentos. Great with chicken, shrimp, pork, beef, sweet potatoes, grilled vegetables, orzo pasta, or other small pasta. Use as a marinade or as a sauce plated under or over foods. Also a great gift idea for friends.
Serves 12

In a medium sauce pan, sweat the onion and garlic on low heat with vegetable cooking spray. Add the paprika and roasted red bell pepper. Cook for 1-2 minutes. Add the crushed tomato, brown sugar, then balsamic vinegar. Cook barbecue sauce for at least 20 minutes and adjust consistency with water, if necessary. Adjust seasoning with salt and pepper, and add green onions before serving.

Calories (kcal)	*50*
Total Fat (gm)	*0*
% Calories from Fat	*3%*
Cholesterol (mg)	*0*
Sodium (mg)	*78*

Roasted Yellow Pepper Sauce

4 yellow bell peppers
¼ cup green onion, chopped
2 tsp. garlic, minced
½ cup cilantro, chopped
2 tbsp. lime juice
1 tsp. lime zest
1 cup low-fat buttermilk
2 tbsp. corn oil
3 tbsp. honey
Salt and pepper

A great sauce to serve with grilled fish, especially salmon, as well as chicken or steak. The color accents the appearance of so many foods.
Serves 8

Char yellow bell peppers over an open flame. Place in a bowl and cover for 5 minutes. Peel the black char and skins from the peppers and rinse. Remove the seeds, core, and membranes from peppers.

Place the roasted peppers, onion, garlic, cilantro, lime, lime zest, buttermilk, oil, and honey in a blender. Puree until smooth.

Calories (kcal)	100
Total Fat (gm)	4
% Calories from Fat	33%
Cholesterol (mg)	1
Sodium (mg)	38

Saffron Aioli

2 tbsp. shallots, minced
3 tsp. garlic, minced
Pinch saffron threads
1 cup dry white wine
1 cup fat-free mayonnaise
3 tbsp. lemon juice
Salt and pepper, to taste

This is wonderful drizzled over chicken, fish, shrimp, vegetables, and especially poached eggs at breakfast. Feel free to adjust the consistency to your liking with a little vegetable stock or water.
Serves 12

In a small sauce pan, heat the shallots, garlic, saffron, and white wine. Reduce by half. Transfer to a stainless bowl and whisk into mayonnaise and lemon juice. Season with salt and pepper.

Calories (kcal)	30
Total Fat (gm)	0
% Calories from Fat	0
Cholesterol (mg)	0
Sodium (mg)	168

Sun-Dried Tomato Pesto

8 oz. sun-dried tomatoes
2 cups warm water
¼ cup almonds, toasted
3 cloves garlic
3 tbsp. Parmesan cheese, grated
¼ cup white wine
⅔ cup parsley, chopped
Salt and pepper, to taste

A great accompaniment for sandwiches or canapés. Also great lightly spread on a pizza round, topped with vegetables.
Serves 8

Place tomatoes in warm water for at least 20 minutes. Place reconstituted tomatoes and their juices in a food processor. Blend with almonds, garlic, cheese, and wine. Puree until smooth. Remove and fold with parsley. Season with salt and pepper.

Calories (kcal)	119
Total Fat (gm)	4
% Calories from Fat	26%
Cholesterol (mg)	1
Sodium (mg)	639

Vegetable Marinara

1 tbsp. olive oil
1 cup onion, chopped
3 tbsp. garlic, chopped
½ cup carrot, chopped
2 tbsp. tomato paste
1 cup cabernet sauvignon
½ cup mushroom, sliced
3 cups diced tomatoes, with juice
1 bay leaf
1 sprig rosemary
½ cup green onion
¼ cup basil
¼ cup parsley
Cracked red pepper, to taste
Black pepper, to taste

A fantastic, well-rounded tomato marinara to be used with pastas, poultry, and seafood. The consistency should be thick and chunky. If a thinner sauce is desired, chop the vegetables finer and thin slightly with tomato sauce.
Serves 12

Heat olive oil in a medium sauce pan. Sauté onion and garlic for 3 minutes until brown and caramelized. Add the carrot and continue browning vegetables. Add tomato paste and stir until well combined. Cook for 1 minute to caramelize the tomato before adding wine. Cook sauce for 5 minutes, or until strong wine flavor softens. Add mushrooms and tomatoes with juice. Season with bay and rosemary sprig and allow to simmer for 20 minutes on low heat. Add green onions, basil, and parsley, and season to taste with pepper.

Calories (kcal)	56
Total Fat (gm)	2
% Calories from Fat	28%
Cholesterol (mg)	0
Sodium (mg)	66

CHAPTER 10

Rice, Potatoes, and Sides

Creamy Polenta
Curried Fried Rice
Fusilli Pasta with Onion Sauce
Holiday Wild Rice
Horseradish Mashed Potatoes
Maque Choux
Mushroom and Asparagus Risotto
Oyster Dressing
Peppered Spoon Bread
Skillet Browned Potatoes
Southwestern Cornsticks
Spinach Gnocchi
Steamed Spinach with Garlic
Summer Fresh Creamed Corn
Tasso and Spinach Pierogi

Creamy Polenta

1½ cups polenta
¾ cup salt
5 cups water
1 clove garlic, mashed

Calories (kcal)	95
Total Fat (gm)	0.4
% Calories from Fat	4%
Cholesterol (mg)	0
Sodium (mg)	605

If a true polenta meal is not available, substitute with cornmeal. Drizzle with extra virgin olive oil and sprinkle Parmesan cheese for a delightful garnish. Serve with any type and style of meat such as beef, veal, or lamb. This is also good with robust-flavored fish such as salmon.
Serves 8

Combine the polenta, salt, water, and garlic in a sauce pan. Stirring constantly with a wooden spoon scrapping the bottom of the pan, heat to a boil. Reduce heat and cook uncovered for 10 minutes, stirring frequently.

Curried Fried Rice

1½ tbsp. sesame oil
3 cups onion, chopped
¼ cup garlic, chopped
1⅓ tbsp. jalapeno, minced
2 cups carrot, diced
1 quart frozen green peas, defrosted
1⅓ cups low-sodium chicken broth
1⅓ tbsp. curry powder
2 tsp. cumin, ground
1½ quarts cooked rice, chilled
Salt and pepper, to taste
Vegetable cooking spray
8 eggs, slightly beaten

Enjoy this as a side dish or as a flavorful vegetarian entree.
Serves 12

Heat oil in a large sauté pan or wok. Add the onion and garlic. Stir-fry for 1 minute. Add the carrot and pepper. Stir-fry an additional minute. Add the peas and rice, stir fry until warm, add broth, and season with salt and pepper. Stir-fry until moist and rice still breaks to the touch. Remove from the wok. Wipe the skillet clean. While still hot add the egg. Cook until almost set. Turn and finish cooking the "egg pancake." Remove and chop into pieces. Add to rice.

Calories (kcal)	250
Total Fat (gm)	5
% Calories from Fat	19%
Cholesterol (mg)	133
Sodium (mg)	158

Fusilli Pasta with Onion Sauce

3 tbsp. olive oil
4 cups yellow onion, thinly sliced
5 anchovies
¾ cup white wine
1 head radicchio, shaved
Salt and pepper, to taste
1 lb. fusilli pasta

Calories (kcal)	306
Total Fat (gm)	6
% Calories from Fat	20%
Cholesterol (mg)	2
Sodium (mg)	100

An onion sauce is a very traditional sauce for pasta throughout Italy. It is also a great example of how simplicity in a recipe can be elegant.
Serves 8

Heat olive oil in a large skillet until hot. Add the onions and cook until caramelized, about 15 minutes, stirring occasionally. Add the wine to onions and reduce for 5 minutes. Add the anchovies and slightly mash into the sauce. Hold warm to the side. Bring a large pot of water to a rolling boil. Cook the pasta until tender and drain, reserving some of the cooking water.

Add the radicchio to the onion sauce and allow to wilt. Toss the pasta with the sauce, adding enough of the pasta cooking water to moisten and thicken.

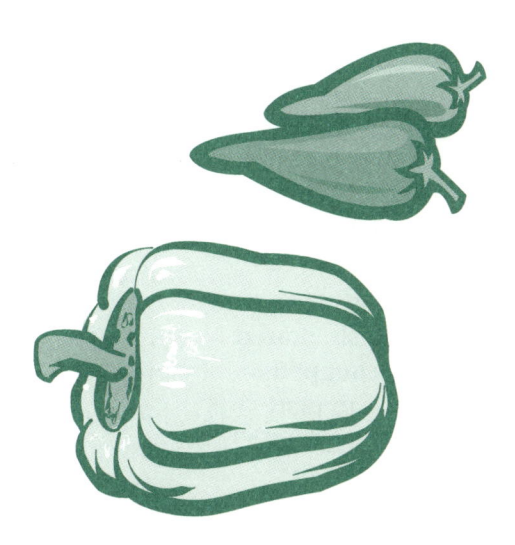

Holiday Wild Rice

1 cup white rice
½ cup wild rice
3½ cups low-sodium beef broth, or chicken stock
1 tbsp. parsley, chopped
½ cup onion, chopped
1 tbsp. garlic, chopped
¾ cup pecans, toasted and crushed
¾ cup golden seedless raisins
¾ cup green onion, chopped

Succulent fruit and nuts add great flavor to this side dish. Serve with roast turkey, ham, or any other holiday meat dish.
Serves 6

Wash the white rice until the water runs clear. Place in a medium sauce pan with 2 cups of the beef broth, onion, and garlic. Bring to a simmer, cover, and cook 25 minutes. In a separate sauce pan, place wild rice and remaining 1½ cups beef broth. Bring to a simmer, cover, and cook for 45 minutes, or until each wild rice grain has split. If not all of the broth is absorbed, drain. In a large casserole dish, fold together the white rice, wild rice, toasted pecans, raisins, and green onion. Cover and warm in a 300-degree oven for 10 minutes.

Calories (kcal)	283
Total Fat (gm)	5
% Calories from Fat	15%
Cholesterol (mg)	0
Sodium (mg)	361

Horseradish Mashed Potatoes

4 russet potatoes, washed and peeled
½ cup evaporated skim milk
2 tbsp. margarine
3 tbsp. horseradish, grated
2 tbsp. chives, chopped
Salt and pepper, to taste

Horseradish will lose some of its spicy flavor when heated. Therefore, if you prepare these potatoes ahead of time, wait and fold in the horseradish just before serving. Serve with grilled salmon, lean roast beef, or steaks.
Serves 6

Peel the potatoes and cut into large, consistent-sized chunks. Place in a sauce pan with cold water rising just to the top of the potatoes. Bring to a simmer and cook until potatoes are tender, about 5 minutes. Drain and lay out on a sheet pan to steam dry any extra moisture for 2 minutes. Whip the potatoes

Rice, Potatoes, and Sides

Calories (kcal)	81
Total Fat (gm)	2
% Calories from Fat	23%
Cholesterol (mg)	1
Sodium (mg)	58

in a mixer with evaporated skim milk and margarine. Be careful not to over whip the potatoes, causing them to become gluey. With a spoon, fold in the horseradish and chives.

Maque Choux

- 1 tbsp. olive oil
- ½ cup onion, chopped
- 3 tbsp. garlic, minced
- ½ cup carrot, medium dice
- ½ cup corn kernels
- 1 cup black-eyed peas
- 1 cup chicken stock, or low-sodium broth
- ¾ cup tomato, seeded and chopped
- 2 tbsp. fresh thyme

A wonderful side dish for any menu, but also a unique salsa or garnish for grilled seafood, crab cakes, or roast chicken breasts. Serves 6

Sauté the onion and garlic in olive oil. Add the carrot and corn, and cook another minute. Add the black-eyed peas and chicken broth. Cook for 5-7 minutes, or until peas are tender. Add the tomato and thyme and serve.

Calories (kcal)	153
Total Fat (gm)	3
% Calories from Fat	17%
Cholesterol (mg)	0
Sodium (mg)	192

Mushroom and Asparagus Risotto

½ cup dried mushrooms, soak in 1 cup water
1½ cups risotto or aborio rice
1 tbsp. garlic, minced
½ cup onion, minced
1 cup white wine
2 cups chicken stock, or low-sodium broth
1 cup asparagus, steamed
¾ cup Asiago cheese

Calories (kcal)	391
Total Fat (gm)	9
% Calories from Fat	23%
Cholesterol (mg)	26
Sodium (mg)	675

When cooked, the risotto should still be firm yet cooked in the center. The reason for stirring the rice while it cooks is to develop this creamy glistening texture from the starches in the rice. Risotto is a dish that should be served immediately after it is prepared. Great for a small get-together, and the kids will love it. Serves 6

Place the dried mushrooms in a cup of warm water and let sit for 10 minutes. Warm stock over stove or in microwave. Combine the aborio rice, onion, garlic, and white wine in a sauce pan. Place on medium heat, stirring constantly, and cook until wine is almost absorbed. Add the stock ½ cup at a time, stirring constantly until adsorbed. Add the mushrooms with the flavored water, and cook a further 2 minutes. Add ½ cup of the cheese and half the asparagus. Plate and garnish with remaining cheese and asparagus.

Oyster Dressing

1 pint oysters
Vegetable cooking spray
½ cup onion, chopped
1 tbsp. garlic, minced
¼ cup celery, chopped
¼ cup green bell pepper, chopped
¼ cup red bell pepper, chopped
3 cups fresh bread crumbs

To make fresh bread crumbs, tear a fresh loaf of bread into pieces and pulse in a food processor. The crumbs are soft, rather than stale or dried. One-half loaf of sandwich bread will yield about 3 cups of fresh bread crumbs. Serve with any poultry menu, but this recipe is also wonderful with fresh grilled fish or shellfish. Serves 6

Preheat an oven to 350 degrees. Strain oysters from their juices, reserving the liquid. Heat a large sauté pan over medium heat. Add the oysters and barely poach, about 4 minutes. Remove to a large mixing bowl. Spray the pan with vegetable cooking spray and sauté the onion and garlic for 1 minute.

3 tsp. thyme
1 tsp. sage, chopped
1 tsp. savory, chopped
1 tsp. lemon zest
Cracked black pepper, to taste
2 tbsp. olive oil

Add the celery and bell pepper and cook a further 3-4 minutes. Transfer sautéed vegetables to mixing bowl. Add the fresh bread crumbs, thyme, sage, savory, lemon zest, and juice from the oysters. Season to taste with pepper, and transfer to a baking dish. Bake for 30-35 minutes uncovered. Remove from oven and drizzle with olive oil.

Calories (kcal)	*41*
Total Fat (gm)	*1*
% Calories from Fat	*13%*
Cholesterol (mg)	*0*
Sodium (mg)	*106*

Peppered Spoon Bread

1½ cups cornmeal, or polenta
1 quart milk
½ red bell pepper, seeded and diced
½ poblano pepper, seeded and diced
½ medium red onion, chopped
Salt, to taste
Pinch cayenne
3 eggs, separated
⅓ cup Parmesan cheese, grated

If you have never tried spoon bread, it is best described as polenta soufflé. Serve this with roasted chicken or pan-fried trout. Serve the meat over the bread, then pour a little of the juices on top to soak into the bread. Delicious!
Serves 6

Preheat oven to 350 degrees. Separate eggs. Whip egg whites to soft peaks. Combine the milk, peppers, and onion in a medium sauce pan. Heat until warm. Add the cornmeal and stir until cornmeal is soft, about 10-15 minutes. Season the cornmeal to taste with salt and pepper. Add a little of the hot cornmeal to the egg yolks to temper, then add the yolks back to the cornmeal mixture. Pour the mixture into a bowl. Gently fold the whipped egg whites into the corn mash. Mixture should be fluffy and light. Spray an 8-by-8-inch pan with vegetable spray. Pour the mixture into pans. Sprinkle with grated cheese. Bake for 20 minutes, or until fluffy and brown on top. Serve as soon as possible.

Calories(kcal)	*286*
Total Fat (gm)	*10*
% Calories from Fat	*30%*
Cholesterol (mg)	*116*
Sodium (mg)	*13*

Skillet Browned Potatoes

2 lb. new potatoes, cubed
2 tbsp. olive oil
1 cup onion, chopped
1 tbsp. garlic, minced
1 tsp. oregano
½ tbsp. kosher salt
2 tbsp. basil, chopped

A black cast-iron skillet is special in that it can hold heat so well. It can brown foods and roast foods at the same time. These potatoes are perfect for the cook who needs quick ideas for after-work meals. Serve potatoes straight out of the skillet.
Serves 6

Preheat an oven to 350 degrees. Heat a black cast-iron skillet over medium heat. Add the oil, onion, garlic, and oregano. Cook for 1 minute, then toss potatoes in seasoned pan. Place in oven and roast uncovered for 30 minutes, or until potatoes are tender. Remove from oven, and toss potatoes with basil.

Calories(kcal)	286
Total Fat (gm)	10
% Calories from Fat	30%
Cholesterol (mg)	116
Sodium (mg)	13

Southwestern Cornsticks

1½ tsp. vegetable oil
¾ cup red bell pepper, chopped
¼ cup onion, chopped
2 tsp. garlic, chopped
¾ cup flour
¾ cup yellow cornmeal
1½ tbsp. sugar
2 tsp. baking powder
¼ tsp. baking soda
¼ tsp. salt
¾ cup frozen corn kernels, defrosted
1 cup non-fat buttermilk
1 egg, lightly beaten
Vegetable cooking spray

Fantastic served with chili on a cold night. My grandmother would serve warm with cold syrup on top when I was a child.
Serves 8

Preheat oven to 400 degrees. Sauté the bell pepper, onion, and garlic in vegetable oil for 2 minutes or until just soft. Combine the flour, cornmeal, sugar, baking powder, baking soda, and salt. Mix well. Add the sautéed vegetables and corn. Again, mix well. Make a well in the center of mixture. Combine buttermilk and eggs; stir well. Add to dry ingredients, stirring just until dry ingredients are moistened. Spray cast-iron cornstick pans with vegetable cooking spray and place into oven until very hot. Spoon batter into hot pan, and bake for 20 minutes.

Calories (kcal)	136
Total Fat (gm)	2
% Calories from Fat	13%
Cholesterol (mg)	27
Sodium (mg)	206

Spinach Gnocchi

- 2 russet potatoes, peeled and quartered
- 1 6-oz. package frozen spinach, defrosted
- 1 cup flour
- ¼ cup part-skim ricotta cheese
- ½ tsp. salt
- ⅛ tsp. pepper
- Pinch nutmeg
- 1 egg
- Vegetable cooking spray
- 2 tbsp. extra virgin olive oil
- 2 tbsp. garlic, minced
- 1 cup Roma tomatoes, seeded and chopped
- 2 tbsp. fresh basil, coarsely chopped
- 3 oz. Asiago cheese, grated

There are great starch dishes other than pasta, rice, and potatoes. Gnocchi are small potato, pasta-like dumplings you are sure to love. Feel free to make extra, and freeze before boiling. Serves 8

Steam potatoes in a basket over 1 cup of water until tender, about 20 minutes. Allow to air dry and cool. Mash potatoes smooth. Press from the spinach any excess moisture and finely chop.

In a mixer on low speed, combine the mashed potatoes, spinach, ½ cup flour, ricotta, salt, pepper, nutmeg, and egg into a dough. Do not over mix. Place on a clean, floured surface and knead in remaining flour. Divide into 4 portions and roll into a rope about an inch in diameter. Using a tablespoon, scoop a spoonful off the rope at an angle, creating a concave-shaped dumpling. Place on a sheet pan coated with cooking spray. Repeat for the rest of the dough.

Bring a large pot of salted water to a boil. Cook the gnocci for about 2 minutes. Unlike pasta, gnocchi are best tested by taste rather than by texture. They should be just firm, but primarily taste cooked (not a raw, starchy flavor). Lift out of the water with a slotted spoon. Toss the hot gnocchi with olive oil, garlic, tomato, basil, and cheese.

Calories (kcal)	226
Total Fat (gm)	8
% Calories from Fat	32%
Cholesterol (mg)	38
Sodium (mg)	289

Steamed Spinach with Garlic

1½ lb. fresh spinach
1 tbsp. extra virgin olive oil
4 cloves garlic, mashed
Salt and pepper, to taste
½ lemon, juiced

Fresh steamed spinach will give a flavor no frozen product can, and is so easy to prepare for any dish. The amount to use can be confusing, since the fresh spinach reduces to such a small amount after it has wilted. A good rule of thumb: A store-bought bag of spinach usually steams down to 3-4 servings (about 10-12 oz. if fresh). Prepare in batches, since a large sauté pan will still only give 3-4 servings.
Serves 8

To clean spinach, fill a bowl or tub with water. Plunge spinach in water and lift out. Gently shake any excess water from the spinach, but you need not dry it completely. What little moisture still holds to the leaves will provide the water for steaming. Pick out any yellow or badly bruised leaves. Remove stems and any thick center veins.

Heat a large sauté pan with olive oil on medium heat. Add the mashed garlic and sauté until garlic begins to just get brown and has seasoned the oil. Add the spinach. Using tongs, lightly turn in the pan to wilt. When all spinach has wilted, season with salt and pepper and lemon juice.

Calories (kcal)	37
Total Fat (gm)	2
% Calories from Fat	40%
Cholesterol (mg)	0
Sodium (mg)	68

Summer Fresh Creamed Corn

6 ears of corn
½ tsp. olive oil
¼ cup milk
1 tsp. thyme
Pinch salt and pepper

Calories (kcal)	54
Total Fat (gm)	1
% Calories from Fat	20%
Cholesterol (mg)	1
Sodium (mg)	13

Sweet corn is definitely a flavor of summer! Serve with sliced tomatoes and barbecued chicken using Roasted Pepper Barbecue Sauce (see recipe).
Serves 6

Remove the silk and husks from the corn, and discard. Holding the ear of corn upright, cut the kernels from the cob, making sure not to cut into the cob or cut too closely. Repeat for the rest of the ears of corn, then chop kernels and place in a bowl. Go back to the cobs and, again, hold upright on the cutting board. Using the sharp edge of your knife tilted at an angle, scrape the cobs to remove the "milk" and germ of the corn. The milk is the sweet, milky liquid left from the kernels. Collect all of the scrapings, and add to the bowl of kernels. In a medium sauce pan, heat olive oil. Add corn kernels, milk (corn), milk (dairy), and thyme. Cook for 10 minutes on low heat. Season with salt and pepper.

Tasso and Spinach Pierogi

2 cups spinach, chopped fine
⅓ cup tasso ham, minced
4 russet potatoes, peeled and diced
1 tbsp. cracked black pepper
1 lb. pizza dough, frozen
12 oz. Marinara Sauce, recipe in book

Calories (kcal)	272
Total Fat (gm)	5
% Calories from Fat	15%
Cholesterol (mg)	6
Sodium (mg)	561

Make your own pizza dough or look for it in the frozen section of your grocery. A great appetizer or entree that everyone loves, especially the kids.
Serves 6

Clean and chop spinach, then place spinach in a mixing bowl for stuffing. Peel and dice the potatoes. Steam over the stove until tender and mash fine. Add mashed potatoes to the spinach and ½ cup tasso ham. Fold together. Allow dough to defrost and roll out on a clean surface. Using a biscuit cutter, cut 12 circular rounds out of pastry. Stuff the pierogis by placing 1-2 tbsp. of potato filling in the center of the disk and fold over. Crimp the edges to seal. Place on a sheet pan and bake for 15 minutes, turning half way through cooking. Serve pierogis with Marinara Sauce.

CHAPTER 11

Desserts and Sweets

Apple Bread Pudding with Bourbon Hard Sauce
Apple Pie with Cinnamon Streusel Topping
Blue Corn Berry Pudding
Carrot Cake
Chocolate Raspberry Napoleons
Corn and Maple Pudding
Couer à la Creme
Frozen Hot Chocolate
Ginger Bread with Brandied Cherry-Orange Sauce
Key Lime Pie with Dark Chocolate Crust
Lemon Gelati
Mango Ice with Pistachios
Mocha Cafe au Lait Cake
Peach Berry Shortcake à la Mode
Pear and Almond Tart
Sweet Cheese Crepes with Cherries Jubilee

Apple Bread Pudding with Bourbon Hard Sauce

1 loaf French bread
2 Granny Smith apples, cored and chopped
1 cup sugar
½ tsp. nutmeg
1 tsp. vanilla
4 eggs
1½ cups skim milk
6 tbsp. butter
1 cup sugar
½ cup water
½ cup bourbon
Vegetable cooking spray

In Louisiana, an establishment's bread pudding is often its signature dish. You will be very proud for this delicious and healthful bread pudding to be your signature dish.
Serves 12

Preheat an oven to 350 degrees. Tear bread with crust into pieces the size of small limes. In a large bowl, combine bread, apple, and 1 cup of sugar. Whip eggs, milk, nutmeg, and vanilla in a separate bowl. Pour over bread mixture and gently fold together. Spray a 10-inch spring form pan with cooking spray. Fill the pan with bread custard mixture, then spray top with cooking spray. Bake for 20 minutes. Meanwhile, melt the sugar, butter, water, and bourbon in a small sauce pan. To serve, unmold bread pudding onto a platter and pour the hard sauce over the top.

Calories (kcal)	502
Total Fat (gm)	15
% Calories from Fat	28%
Cholesterol (mg)	152
Sodium (mg)	211

Apple Pie with Cinnamon Streusel Topping

2½ lb. cooking apples
¼ cup light brown sugar, firmly packed
2 tbsp. flour
1 tbsp. vanilla extract
1 pie crust (9-inch)
½ cup light brown sugar
¼ cup flour
¼ cup rolled oats

The type of apple used will determine the personality of your pie. Firm tart apples will give you a crunchy light pie, while a sweet and softer apple will cook down to a sweet and smooth pie. I prefer to use tart Granny Smith apples for this pie, but Rome, Fugi, or Golden Delicious apples are also very good.
Serves 12

Preheat oven to 350 degrees. Core, peel, and slice the apples. Place in a large bowl and add sugar, flour, and vanilla. Toss well to coat. Line a 9-inch pie pan with pastry shell. Spoon

½ tsp. cinnamon, ground
3 tbsp. margarine, cold, cubed

apples into pastry shell, cover with aluminum foil, and bake for 45 minutes.

Meanwhile, combine remaining ½ cup brown sugar, flour, oats, cinnamon, and margarine. Mix well with a fork until crumbly. After pie has baked 45 minutes, remove from oven and sprinkle on the topping. Return to oven and bake an additional 30 minutes.

Calories (kcal)	*252*
Total Fat (gm)	*11*
% Calories from Fat	*38%*
Cholesterol (mg)	*0*
Sodium (mg)	*204*

Blue Corn Berry Pudding

2 cups creamed corn, fresh if possible
1 cup blue corn meal (or yellow)
¾ cup sugar
½ tsp. baking powder
Pinch ground nutmeg
½ cup margarine, melted
1 cup non-fat buttermilk
2 eggs, lightly beaten
Vegetable cooking spray
2 pints blueberries

A great dessert to serve after any Southwestern or native American menu.
Serves 8

In a small sauce pan, bring the blueberries and ½ cup sugar to a simmer and heat for 5 minutes. Remove from heat. Preheat an oven to 425 degrees. In a large bowl, combine the creamed corn, cornmeal, remaining sugar, baking powder, and nutmeg. Fold in the margarine, buttermilk, and egg. Spray an 8-inch cake pan with cooking spray. Pour batter inside, then pour half the blueberry mixture evenly over the batter. Bake for 15 minutes. Remove and allow to cool. Serve at room temperature with remaining blueberry sauce on top.

Calories (kcal)	*352*
Total Fat (gm)	*14*
% Calories from Fat	*33%*
Cholesterol (mg)	*46*
Sodium (mg)	*372*

Carrot Cake

1 cup flour
²/₃ cup sugar
1 tsp. baking soda
Pinch salt
¼ cup plain non-fat yogurt
3 tbsp. canola oil
1 tsp. orange zest
½ tsp. vanilla
2 egg whites
1 cup grated fresh carrots
Vegetable cooking spray
4 oz. Neufchatel cheese, room temperature
¾ cup powdered sugar
¼ tsp. vanilla
2 tbsp. orange zest

This cake has a great rich and dense texture, and is very moist. The trick is not to overcook the cake and dry it out.
Serves 8

Combine the flour, sugar, baking soda, and salt in a mixing bowl. In a separate bowl, combine the yogurt, oil, orange zest, and vanilla. Mix well before adding the grated carrot. Fold the wet ingredients with the dry ingredients.

Preheat an oven to 350 degrees. Spread the batter into an 8-inch spring form pan or cake round that has been sprayed with vegetable cooking spray. Bake for 30 minutes. Allow to cool 10 minutes before removing from the pan. Let cool completely. Using a mixer, combine the cream cheese, powdered sugar, and vanilla. Spoon on top of cake and sprinkle orange zest on top to garnish.

Calories (kcal)	257
Total Fat (gm)	9
% Calories from Fat	30%
Cholesterol (mg)	11
Sodium (mg)	234

Chocolate Raspberry Napoleons

9 sheets filo dough
Vegetable cooking spray
3 tbsp. sugar, for sprinkling
1½ cups fat-free cream cheese
1 cup fat-free sour cream
¾ cup sugar
2 tbsp. Cointreau

Don't be afraid to work with filo dough. Once you have tried it, you will begin using it for all sorts of dishes. It provides a delicate, crunchy pastry for desserts and savory foods alike, but we can regulate how much fat we add.
Serves 6

Preheat an oven to 350 degrees. Lay one filo sheet on a clean working surface. Spray half the sheet with vegetable cooking spray and lightly sprinkle with sugar. Fold the clean half over the sugared half. Spray with cooking spray and sprinkle with sugar. Lay another sheet down. Repeat the layering until 3

¾ cup semisweet chocolate chips, chopped fine
¼ cup skim milk
3 cups raspberries

Calories (kcal)	465
Total Fat (gm)	8
% Calories from Fat	17%
Cholesterol (mg)	17
Sodium (mg)	559

sheets have been layered on top of each other to create a complete napoleon layer of 6 half sheets. Cut into quarters and place on a sheet pan. Prepare 2 more napoleon filo sheet layers and place on sheet pans. Bake in the oven for 25 minutes. Let cool completely.

In a mixer, whip the cream cheese, sour cream, sugar, and Cointreau until light and creamy. Lay a baked napoleon filo layer. Spread a layer of cream on 1 baked napoleon filo layer. Cover with raspberries. Lay another baked napoleon filo layer on top. Spread with cream and cover with raspberries. Lay the final filo layer on top and place in the refrigerator. In a small sauce pan, melt the chocolate with the milk on low heat. To serve, pour chocolate sauce over and top with any remaining raspberries.

Corn and Maple Pudding

1¼ lb. frozen corn kernels, defrosted
2 cups skim milk
¼ cup flour
¼ cup maple syrup
½ tsp. salt
½ tsp. nutmeg, ground
6 egg whites
4 whole eggs
1½ cups grated carrots
Vegetable cooking spray

Serve warm, cold, or at room temperature. The carrot puree is the trick to maintaining good moisture and thus good flavor in this dish.
Serves 8

Preheat oven to 350 degrees. Press any excess moisture from the corn. Puree the corn, milk, and flour in a food processor. In a separate bowl, mix the syrup, salt, nutmeg, egg whites, eggs, carrot, and corn puree until thoroughly combined. Pour into a 1-quart Pyrex casserole pan sprayed with cooking spray. Bake for 15 minutes covered with foil. Remove foil and continue baking 30 minutes or until set. Spoon into parfait glasses and drizzle with maple syrup.

Calories (kcal)	183
Total Fat (gm)	3
% Calories from Fat	16%
Cholesterol (mg)	107
Sodium (mg)	248

Couer à la Creme

- 8 oz. fat-free cream cheese
- 8 oz. cottage cheese, lowfat
- 1 cup sugar
- 1 tbsp. vanilla
- 6 oz. whipping cream
- 1½ cups raspberries
- 1 cup strawberries, washed, stemmed, cut

The rich, gooey, gooey desserts are not always the best. Remember that simplicity is elegant leading to the decadent. This dessert is the perfect example.
Serves 6

Mix cheeses together in a blender until smooth. Gradually add sugar and vanilla. Remove to a bowl and fold in cream. Pour into a sieve lined with cheesecloth. Set on top of a bowl to drain, and refrigerate for 12 hours. Line a heart-shaped mold with cheesecloth. Pack mixture in and chill overnight. Turn out onto a platter and cover with fresh strawberries and raspberries.

Calories (kcal)	239
Total Fat (gm)	8
% Calories from Fat	32%
Cholesterol (mg)	35
Sodium (mg)	278

Frozen Hot Chocolate

- ⅔ cup unsweetened cocoa powder
- 1 cup sugar
- 1 quart whole milk

A great idea for a fun summer dessert. Serve in cocoa mugs and garnish with a side of your favorite liqueurs.
Serves 8

Place cocoa powder, sugar, and milk in a sauce pan. Cook on low heat until sugar dissolves. Pour into ice cube trays. Freeze overnight. Blend cubes in a blender and serve to order.

Calories (kcal)	188
Total Fat (gm)	5
% Calories from Fat	22%
Cholesterol (mg)	17
Sodium (mg)	62

Gingerbread with Brandied Cherry-Orange Sauce

6 oranges
½ cup cherries, pitted and halved
1 cup orange juice, strained
½ cup sugar
3 tbsp. kirsch, or cherry brandy
1 cinnamon stick
¼ cup water
½ cup butter, softened
1½ cups sugar
2 eggs
1 cup applesauce
1 tsp. vanilla
2 cups flour
2 tsp. baking soda
½ tsp. cinnamon
⅛ tsp. allspice
⅛ tsp. ginger
½ cup buttermilk

For additional flavor, grind your own spices. In this case, break up the cinnamon stick into a spice grinder with whole allspice and grind to a fine powder. You may then toast over a small flame to release even more flavor.
Serves 12

Remove the skins from the oranges and slice into wheels. Place in a bowl with cherries. In a medium sauce pan, combine the orange juice, sugar, brandy, water, and cinnamon stick. Bring to a simmer, flame, and cook for 2 minutes. Pour over the oranges and cherries, and remove cinnamon stick. Let sit for 30 minutes in cooler.

In a mixer, whip the butter and sugar until light and fluffy. Add the eggs and vanilla and continue whipping. Incorporate the flour, spices, and buttermilk and mix for 3 minutes to fully combine. Pour into prepared 8½-by-11-inch cake pan. Bake at 350 degrees for 35 minutes. Remove from oven and allow to cool. With a paring knife, dot the cake with cuts straight into the cake. Pour the orange liquor into holes to soak into cake. Serve soaked ginger bread with brandied oranges.

Calories (kcal)	354
Total Fat (gm)	9
% Calories from Fat	22%
Cholesterol (mg)	51
Sodium (mg)	310

Key Lime Pie with Dark Chocolate Crust

1 cup chocolate wafer cookies, crumbled fine
¼ cup sugar
1 tbsp. butter, melted
½ cup fresh lime juice
2 tsp. lime zest
3 tbsp. flour
3 eggs, separated
2 tbsp. butter
¼ cup water
2 egg whites
½ cup sugar

Calories (kcal)	281
Total Fat (gm)	10
% Calories from Fat	32%
Cholesterol (mg)	80
Sodium (mg)	249

Key lime pie is named for the small sweet limes found around the Florida Keys. These limes are not always available, but we can make sure that we are choosing the ripest and sweetest limes from our grocer. For limes, the greener is not the better! Ripe sweet limes will have thinner skins, be yellowing slightly, and have a pleasant lime aroma when you smell and pierce their skins.
Serves 6-8

Combine the chocolate cookie wafers, butter, and tbsp. of sugar. Press into bottom of 9-inch pie pan. The mixture will be more crumbly than most pie crusts but will be more firm after chilling. In a medium bowl, combine the lime juice, lime zest, flour, 3 egg yolks, 2 tbsp. butter, and water. Cook over a double broiler until it thickens. Pour into pie shell. Allow to chill in cooler for 1 hour. Whip the 5 egg whites and ½ cup sugar in a mixer until soft peaks form. Lightly spoon onto the filling. Bake in a 375-degree oven until lightly brown. Chill before serving.

Lemon Gelati

1½ cups sugar
1½ tbsp. lemon zest
1½ dashes salt
1 cup fresh lemon juice
2½ cups plain non-fat yogurt, room temperature
⅓ cup fresh mint, chopped

Gelati is the name for Italian-style ice cream. This light and delicate ice cream is perfect after a very rich meal, or as a midday snack when the weather is hot.
Serves 8

Combine the sugar, zest, salt, and lemon juice. Stir until sugar has dissolved. Add the yogurt and mix well. Pour into an ice cream freezer and prepare as machine instructs. Garnish with fresh mint.

Calories	*195*
Total Fat (gm)	*0.2*
% Calories from Fat	*1%*
Cholesterol (mg)	*1*
Sodium (mg)	*106*

Mango Ice with Pistachios

2 cups non-fat plain yogurt
2 tbsp. lemon juice
½ tsp. vanilla
1 quart mango, pitted, skinned, mash
½ cup sugar
1 tsp. cinnamon
½ cup pistachio nuts, dry-roasted, toasted

Many fruits, such as ripe mangos, peaches, and bananas, have a natural silkiness. By using these fruits in frozen yogurts, we obtain a "cream-like" texture. Serve this wonderful mango ice as the finale for any Southwestern, Caribbean, or Asian menu.
Serves 6

Combine the yogurt, lemon juice, and vanilla. In another bowl, combine the mango, cinnamon, and sugar, and allow to sit 30 minutes. Fold the ingredients together, then freeze in an ice cream freezer. In the last stages of freezing, add the pistachios.

Calories (kcal)	*193*
Total Fat (gm)	*3*
% Calories from Fat	*15%*
Cholesterol (mg)	*1*
Sodium (mg)	*60*

Mocha Cafe au Lait Cake

½ cup butter
⅔ cup sugar, extra fine
Pinch of salt
2 tbsp. honey
1 tsp. baking powder
1½ cups flour, sifted
3 eggs
1 tsp. vanilla extract
8 oz. fat-free sour cream
16 oz. fat-free cream cheese
1 tsp. nutmeg, ground
2 cups dark roast coffee, brewed
3 tbsp. sugar
1 oz. brandy
2 tbsp. cocoa
½ cup semisweet chocolate, shaved

Inspired by the ever so popular tiramisu, this light and flavorful cake adds a finishing touch to a special menu.
Serves 12

Heat an oven to 375 degrees. Sift flour with baking powder and reserve. In a mixer, whip the butter and sugar for 5 minutes, or until light and fluffy and not gritty. Add the honey and a pinch of salt. Add the baking powder, flour, and eggs one at a time. Flavor with vanilla and pour into an 8-inch spring form pan. Bake for 45 minutes, or until it springs to the touch. Meanwhile, whip the sour cream, cream cheese, nutmeg, and ½ cup sugar until smooth and creamy. Also, melt 3 tbsp. sugar and cocoa into coffee with brandy. Once cake has cooled, cut horizontally into 2 layers. Place 1 layer on a cake plate. Soak the cake layer with coffee mixture, layer with cream cheese filling, then sprinkle with chocolate. Repeat for the top layer.

Calories (kcal)	307
Total Fat (gm)	11
% Calories from Fat	33%
Cholesterol (mg)	74
Sodium (mg)	353

Peach Berry Shortcake à la Mode

Vegetable cooking spray
2 cups flour
1 tbsp. baking powder
⅓ cup soft margarine
1 quart fat-free frozen vanilla yogurt
½ cup sugar
½ cup lemon juice

Many times two great flavors that are in season at the same time always seem to taste great together . . . like tomatoes and basil, shrimp and corn, and, as we see here, blueberries and peaches.
Serves 12

In a bowl, combine flour, baking powder, salt, and sugar. Cut in margarine with 2 knives or a pastry blender. Stir in milk, lemon zest, and lemon juice. Drop batter by teaspoon on prepared cookie sheet. Bake for 10-12 minutes, or until fluffy and golden

2 tbsp. lemon zest
1 cup milk
4 cups peaches, skinned and chopped
½ cup sugar
1 cup blueberries

brown. Place peaches and sugar in medium sauce pan on low heat. Cook for 10 minutes, stirring occasionally. Add the blueberries, and cook an additional minute until berries plump but do not break down. Cut the shortcake biscuits in half, spoon peaches and berries inside, and cover with top of shortcake. Serve ⅓ cup of frozen yogurt on the side with any remaining peach-berry sauce.

Calories (kcal)	286
Total Fat (gm)	6
% Calories from Fat	18%
Cholesterol (mg)	3
Sodium (mg)	214

Pear and Almond Tart

5 sheets filo dough
Vegetable cooking spray
4 oz. Neufchatel cheese, room temperature
½ cup sugar
½ cup almonds, ground
1 tsp. vanilla
2 egg whites
4 pears
3 tbsp. honey
½ cup sugar

The classic name for this popular tart is a Frangipane tart, known for its ground almonds or almond paste. For a variation to the recipe, you may substitute apples for the pears.
Serves 8

Spray a 9-inch tart pan with vegetable cooking spray. Lay a sheet of filo dough into the pan. Spray with cooking spray. Place another sheet into pan. Spray with cooking spray. Repeat this process for all 5 sheets of dough, allowing the dough to fall over the edges of the pan. Cut the edges and crimp decoratively around the edge. Place in refrigerator.

In a mixer, cream the cheese, sugar, almonds, vanilla, and egg whites. Spread into bottom of tart shell. Peel and halve the pears. Remove the core and seeds. Slice pears and arrange into a spiral around the tart. Sprinkle with remaining ½ cup sugar. Bake for 45 minutes in oven. Drizzle with honey.

Calories (kcal)	300
Total Fat (gm)	9
% Calories from Fat	26%
Cholesterol (mg)	11
Sodium (mg)	129

Sweet Cheese Crepes with Cherries Jubilee

3 eggs
2 tbsp. flour
3 tbsp. skim milk
Pinch salt
Pinch sugar
1 lb. fat-free cream cheese, or Neufchatel cheese
½ cup sugar
1 tsp. lemon zest
1 tsp. vanilla
2 pints cherries, pitted
½ cup sugar
1 tbsp. lemon juice
2 oz. kirsch liquor

Kirsch is a true fruit brandy made with cherries. By using the liqueur, flavor and aroma are intensified for such a low-fat dessert.
Serves 6

Place the eggs, flour, milk, salt, and sugar in a blender. Blend until smooth, place in a bowl, and let sit in refrigerator for 10 minutes. Meanwhile, whip the cream cheese, ½ cup sugar, lemon zest, and vanilla until smooth. To make the cherry sauce, combine the cherries, sugar, lemon juice, and liquor in a sauce pan. Heat on low, stirring occasionally, for 10 minutes. Heat a crepe pan or skillet with vegetable cooking spray. Add 3 tbsp. of crepe batter to the pan, and roll pan to distribute batter into a thin pancake. Cook until 1 side is golden brown. Do not flip, but remove from the pan. It helps to flip the pan upside down and allow the crepe to fall onto a plate. Repeat for 6 good crepes. Roll ½ cup of filling into each crepe and pour the cherry sauce on top.

Calories (kcal)	324
Total Fat (gm)	3
% Calories from Fat	8%
Cholesterol (mg)	102
Sodium (mg)	445

Index

Index

a

Apple Bread Pudding with Bourbon Hard Sauce, 168
Apple Pie with Cinnamon Streusel Topping, 168
Apple-Spiced French Toast, 30
Appetizers
    Avocado and Citrus Canapé, 14
    Barbecued Oysters, 14
    Black Bean Tart with Chili Crust, 15
    Brie and Pear Torte, 16
    Caviar Crisps, 16
    Crab-Stuffed Artichoke, 17
    Grilled Shrimp Baha Rolls, 18
    Grilled Zucchini Spears, 18
    Kale and Tasso Pastries, 19
    Lemon Herb Dip, 20
    Louisiana Lump Crabmeat Dip, 20
    Mediterranean Hummus, 21
    Orange Ginger Chicken Sate, 21
    Oysters Louisiane, 22
    Pears with Walnut Cheese, 22
    Poor Man's Caviar with Italian Herbed Crackers, 23
    Smoked Salmon and Endive Canapé, 24
    Spicy Ancho Dip, 24
    Sun-Dried Tomato-Stuffed Mushrooms, 25
    Warm Spinach and Artichoke Dip, 26
    Wild Mushroom Torte, 27
Artichoke Beurre Blanc, 144
Arugula with an Orange Vinaigrette, 40
Avocado and Citrus Canapé, 14

b

Baby Greens Salad with Spring Herb Dressing, 40
Balsamic Vinaigrette, 144
Banana Nut Pancakes, 30
Barbecued Oysters, 14
Barbecued Shrimp with Sweet Corn and Potatoes, 103
Basil Chicken, 86
Beef and Portabella Mushroom Shish Kebab, 128
Black Bean Tart with Chili Crust, 15
Black Bean-Stuffed Sweet Potatoes, 72
Blue Corn Berry Pudding, 169
Bourbon Sweet Onion Sauce, 145
Braised Pork with Sauerkraut and Apples, 128
Brandied Peaches with Sun-Dried Cherries, 146
Breakfast and Brunch
    Apple-Spiced French Toast, 30
    Banana Nut Pancakes, 30
    Broiled Grapefruit with Vanilla Ginger Sugar, 31
    Cafe Brulot, 32
    Eggs Sardou, 32
    Fruit Bagel Pizza, 33
    Garlic Cheese Grits, 34
    Grillades and Garlic Cheese Grits, 34
    Pennington Granola, 35
    Salmon Hash with Horseradish-Dill Cream, 36
    Sweet Potato Pancakes, 36
    Vegetable Frittata, 37

Brie and Pear Torte, 16
Broiled Chiles Rellenos, 72
Broiled Grapefruit with Vanilla Ginger Sugar, 31

C

Cafe Brulot, 32
Cajun Meat Loaf with Smoky Tomato Sauce, 129
Cane-Glazed Chicken Breasts with Leeks and Carrots, 86
Carrot Cake, 170
Caviar Crisps, 16
Champagne Dijon Vinaigrette, 146
Chicken and Black Bean Quesadillas, 87
Chicken and Chive Dumplings, 88
Chicken and Sausage Jambalaya, 88
Chicken Anise, 89
Chicken Curry, 90
Chicken Roulade with Asparagus and Prosciutto, 90
Chicken with Blue Cheese Apples, 91
Chicken with White Beans, 92
Chili Roast with Glazed Tomatoes, 130
Chili Verde, 58
Chilled Pickled Slaw, 41
Chinese Chop Salad, 42
Chocolate Raspberry Napoleons, 170
Corn and Maple Pudding, 171
Corn and Shrimp Chowder with Saged Croutons, 59
Couer à la Creme, 172
Crab Tamales with Ancho Chili Sauce, 104

Crab-Stuffed Artichoke, 17
Crawfish Bisque with Crawfish Croutons, 60
Crawfish Eggrolls, 105
Crawfish Pappardelle with Tomato Brochette, 106
Creamy Dill and Horseradish Potato Salad, 43
Creamy Polenta, 156
Creole Crab Cakes with Roasted Garlic Sauce, 107
Creole Mustard Dressing, 147
Creole Roasted Cornish Hens, 93
Creole Stuffed Bell Peppers, 73
Curried Fried Rice, 156

d

Desserts
   Apple Bread Pudding with Bourbon Hard Sauce, 168
   Apple Pie with Cinnamon Streusel Topping, 168
   Blue Corn Berry Pudding, 169
   Carrot Cake, 170
   Chocolate Raspberry Napoleons, 170
   Corn and Maple Pudding, 171
   Couer à la Creme, 172
   Frozen Hot Chocolate, 172
   Gingerbread with Brandied Cherry-Orange Sauce, 173
   Key Lime Pie with Dark Chocolate Crust, 174
   Lemon Gelati, 175

Mango Ice with Pistachios, 175
Mocha Cafe au Lait Cake, 176
Peach Berry Shortcake à la Mode, 176
Pear and Almond Tart, 177
Sweet Cheese Crepes with Cherries Jubilee, 178
Drum Fish with Johnny Cakes and Creole Red Bell Sauce, 108
Duck and Sausage Cassoulet, 94
Duck Breast with Grilled Radicchio and Sweet Bourbon Oranges, 95

e

Early Spring Blue Crab Salad, 44
Eggs Sardou, 32
El Xochitl (Chicken Soup Fiesta), 70

f

Family-Style Ratatouille over Southern Corn Bread, 74
Fish Soup with Garlic and Escarole, 61
Flank Steak with Olive Tapenade, 130
Frozen Hot Chocolate, 172
Fruit Bagel Pizza, 33
Fusilli Pasta with Onion Sauce, 157

g

Garlic Cheese Grits, 34
Gingerbread with Brandied Cherry-Orange Sauce, 173

Gingered Orange Cranberry Sauce, 147
Grillades and Garlic Cheese Grits, 34
Grilled Lobster and Asparagus with Chervil Butter, 109
Grilled Pork Chops with Calvados Apples, 131
Grilled Shrimp and Curried Lentil Salad, 44
Grilled Shrimp Baha Rolls, 18
Grilled Spring Vegetable Pizza, 74
Grilled Tofu with Olive Tapenade and Preserved Lemons, 75
Grilled Veal Chops with Pear and Green Peppercorn Sauce, 132
Grilled Venison with Roasted Onion Rings, 132
Grilled Zucchini Spears, 18

h

Herbed Ranch Dressing, 148
Herbed Rice Cakes with Red Bean Sauce, 76
Heritage Shepherd's Pie, 77
Hoisin Hoagie, 45
Holiday Turkey with Peppered Dressing, 96
Holiday Wild Rice, 158
Horseradish Mashed Potatoes, 158

i

Italian Bean and Pasta Soup, 62
Italian Muffaletta Sandwich, 46
Italian Vegetable Tart, 78

j

Japanese Noodle Salad, 46

k

Kale and Tasso Pastries, 19
Key Lime Pie with Dark Chocolate Crust, 174

l

Lamb Curry over Basmati Rice, 133
Lamb Stew over White Polenta, 134
Lemon Gelati, 175
Lemon Herb Dip, 20
Lime-Marinated Emu Fajitas with Pumpkin Seeds, 97
Louisiana Lump Crabmeat Dip, 20

m

Mambo Pork Loin and Island Fruits, 134
Mango Ice with Pistachios, 175
Maque Choux, 159
Mardi Gras Salad, 47
Meats
    Beef and Portabella Mushroom Shish Kebab, 128
    Braised Pork with Sauerkraut and Apples, 128
    Cajun Meat Loaf with Smoky Tomato Sauce, 129
    Chili Roast with Glazed Tomatoes, 130
    Flank Steak with Olive Tapenade, 130
    Grilled Pork Chops with Calvados Apples, 131
    Grilled Veal Chops with Pear and Green Peppercorn Sauce, 132
    Grilled Venison with Roasted Onion Rings, 132
    Lamb Curry over Basmati Rice, 133
    Lamb Stew over White Polenta, 134
    Mambo Pork Loin and Island Fruits, 134
    Roast Veal with Pecan Orzo Pasta, 135
    Roasted Pork Loin with Herb Saint Green Sauce, 136
    Rosemary Grilled Leg of Lamb and Vegetables, 137
    Shepherd's Pie, 138
    Spiced Pork Stuffed Bananas, 139
    Veal Roulade with Caper Dressing, 140
    Venison Marsala with Rosemary Sweet Potatoes and Onions, 141
Mediterranean Hummus, 21
Mexican Hominy Stew, 63
Mint Chutney, 148
Minted Far Eastern Marinade, 149
Mocha Cafe au Lait Cake, 176
Mushroom and Artichoke Pasta, 78
Mushroom and Asparagus Risotto, 160

n

Napa Cabbage and Mushroom Sauté, 79
New England Clam Chowder, 64

Index

New England Seafood Pie, 110
Niçoise Pasta Salad, 48

O

Open-Faced Corned Beef Sandwich, 49
Orange Ginger Chicken Sate, 21
Orange Shrimp and Fennel Kabobs, 111
Oyster Dressing, 160
Oysters Louisiane, 22

p

Pan-Roasted Red Snapper with Sherry
   Turtle Sauce, 112
Peach Berry Shortcake à la Mode, 176
Pear and Almond Tart, 177
Pears with Walnut Cheese, 22
Pennington Granola, 35
Peppered Spoon Bread, 161
Pickled Vegetables, 150
Pollo Spanish Rice, 98
Pompano au Papier, 113
Poor Man's Caviar with Italian Herbed
   Crackers, 23
Potato and Leek Soup with Asiago
   Croutons, 65
Poultry
   Basil Chicken, 86
   Cane-Glazed Chicken Breasts with Leeks
     and Carrots, 86
   Chicken and Black Bean Quesadillas, 87
   Chicken and Chive Dumplings, 88
   Chicken and Sausage Jambalaya, 88
   Chicken Anise, 89
   Chicken Curry, 90
   Chicken Roulade with Asparagus and
     Prosciutto, 90
   Chicken with Blue Cheese Apples, 91
   Chicken with White Beans, 92
   Creole Roasted Cornish Hens, 93
   Duck and Sausage Cassoulet, 94
   Duck Breast with Grilled Radicchio and
     Sweet Bourbon Oranges, 95
   Holiday Turkey with Peppered
     Dressing, 96
   Lime-Marinated Emu Fajitas with
     Pumpkin Seeds, 97
   Pollo Spanish Rice, 98
   Simple Szechuan Stir-Fry, 98
   Tandoori Chicken, 99
Pumpkin Velouté, 66

r

Red Bell Tomato Sauce, 150
Remoulade Seafood Dumpling Salad, 50
Roast Veal with Pecan Orzo
   Pasta, 135
Roasted Eggplant with Creole Crawfish, 114
Roasted Garlic, Brie, and Apple
   Sandwich, 51
Roasted Onion and Garlic Salad, 52
Roasted Pepper Barbecue Sauce, 151
Roasted Pork Loin with Herb Saint Green
   Sauce, 136

Roasted Yellow Pepper Sauce, 152
Rosemary Grilled Leg of Lamb and
   Vegetables, 137

S

Saffron Aioli, 152
Saged Roast Duck Salad with Pear
   Vinaigrette, 52
Salads
   Arugula with an Orange Vinaigrette, 40
   Baby Greens Salad with Spring Herb
      Dressing, 40
   Chilled Pickled Slaw, 41
   Chinese Chop Salad, 42
   Creamy Dill and Horseradish Potato
      Salad, 43
   Early Spring Blue Crab Salad, 44
   Grilled Shrimp and Curried
      Lentil Salad, 44
   Japanese Noodle Salad, 46
   Mardi Gras Salad, 47
   Niçoise Pasta Salad, 48
   Remoulade Seafood Dumpling Salad, 50
   Roasted Onion and Garlic Salad, 52
   Saged Roast Duck Salad with Pear
      Vinaigrette, 52
   Southern Vegetable Poboy, 54
   Spinach and Basil Salad with Cajun
      Tasso Vinaigrette, 54
   Summer Tomato Salad, 55
Salmon Hash with Horseradish-Dill
   Cream, 36
Salmon Niçoise, 115

Sandwiches
   Hoisin Hoagie, 45
   Italian Muffaletta Sandwich, 46
   Open-Faced Corned Beef Sandwich, 49
   Roasted Garlic, Brie, and Apple
      Sandwich, 51
   Smoked Salmon and Watercress
      Sandwich, 53
Sauces
   Artichoke Beurre Blanc, 144
   Balsamic Vinaigrette, 144
   Bourbon Sweet Onion Sauce, 145
   Brandied Peaches with Sun-Dried
      Cherries, 146
   Champagne Dijon Vinaigrette, 146
   Creole Mustard Dressing, 147
   Gingered Orange Cranberry Sauce, 147
   Herbed Ranch Dressing, 148
   Mint Chutney, 148
   Minted Far Eastern Marinade, 149
   Pickled Vegetables, 150
   Red Bell Tomato Sauce, 150
   Roasted Pepper Barbecue Sauce, 151
   Roasted Yellow Pepper Sauce, 152
   Saffron Aioli, 152
   Sun Dried Tomato Pesto, 153
   Vegetable Marinara, 154
Scallops in Champagne Sauce over Spring
   Vegetables, 116
Seafood
   Barbecued Shrimp with Sweet Corn and
      Potatoes, 103
   Crab Tamales with Ancho Chili Sauce, 104
   Crawfish Eggrolls, 105

Crawfish Pappardelle with Tomato
   Brochette, 106
Creole Crab Cakes with Roasted Garlic
   Sauce, 107
Drum Fish with Johnny Cakes and
   Creole Red Bell Sauce, 108
Grilled Lobster and Asparagus with
   Chervil Butter, 109
New England Seafood Pie, 110
Orange Shrimp and Fennel Kabobs, 111
Pan-Roasted Red Snapper with Sherry
   Turtle Sauce, 112
Pompano au Papier, 113
Roasted Eggplant with Creole
   Crawfish, 114
Salmon Niçoise, 115
Scallops in Champagne Sauce over
   Spring Vegetables, 116
Seafood Jambalaya, 117
Seared Catfish with Creole Mustard
   Sauce and Dirty Rice, 118
Sizzling Shrimp Fajitas with Confetti
   Peppers, 119
Speckled Trout with Sazerac Sauce, 120
Spiced Moroccan Shrimp over
   Couscous, 121
Spring Trout with Lime Vinaigrette, 122
Steamed Clams and Mussels with Tasso
   Cuisson, 122
Steamed Clams with Cilantro and
   Lime, 123
Swiss Chard Halibut with
   Ginger Sauce, 124
Thai Steamed Mussels, 124

Tuscan Seafood Bake, 125
Seafood Jambalaya, 117
Seared Catfish with Creole Mustard Sauce
   and Dirty Rice, 118
Shepherd's Pie, 138
Side Dishes
   Creamy Polenta, 156
   Curried Fried Rice, 156
   Fusilli Pasta with Onion Sauce, 157
   Holiday Wild Rice, 158
   Horseradish Mashed Potatoes, 158
   Maque Choux, 159
   Mushroom and Asparagus Risotto, 160
   Oyster Dressing, 160
   Peppered Spoon Bread, 161
   Skillet Browned Potatoes, 162
   Southwestern Cornsticks, 162
   Spinach Gnocchi, 163
   Steamed Spinach with Garlic, 164
   Summer Fresh Creamed Corn, 165
   Tasso and Spinach Pierogi, 165
Simple Szechuan Stir-Fry, 98
Sizzling Shrimp Fajitas with Confetti
   Peppers, 119
Skillet Browned Potatoes, 162
Smoked Chicken and Okra Gumbo, 66
Smoked Salmon and Endive Canapé, 24
Smoked Salmon and Watercress
   Sandwich, 53
Soups and Stews
   Chili Verde, 58
   Corn and Shrimp Chowder with Saged
      Croutons, 59
   Crawfish Bisque with Crawfish Croutons, 60

El Xochitl (Chicken Soup Fiesta), 70
Fish Soup with Garlic and Escarole, 61
Italian Bean and Pasta Soup, 62
Mexican Hominy Stew, 63
New England Clam Chowder, 64
Potato and Leek Soup with Asiago Croutons, 65
Pumpkin Velouté, 66
Smoked Chicken and Okra Gumbo, 66
Southwestern Chili, 67
Spinach, Oyster, and Artichoke Soup, 68
Vegetable Orecchiette Soup, 69
Southern Vegetable Poboy, 54
Southwestern Chili, 67
Southwestern Cornsticks, 162
Speckled Trout with Sazerac Sauce, 120
Spiced Moroccan Shrimp over Couscous, 121
Spiced Pork Stuffed Bananas, 139
Spicy Ancho Dip, 24
Spinach and Basil Salad with Cajun Tasso Vinaigrette, 54
Spinach Gnocchi, 163
Spinach, Oyster, and Artichoke Soup, 68
Spring Trout with Lime Vinaigrette, 122
Steamed Clams and Mussels with Tasso Cuisson, 122
Steamed Clams with Cilantro and Lime, 123
Steamed Spinach with Garlic, 164
Stir-Fried Rice Noodles, 80
Stuffed Peppers with Hominy Grits, 80
Summer Fresh Creamed Corn, 165
Summer Squash with Shaved Romano, 81

Summer Tomato Salad, 55
Sun Dried Tomato Pesto, 153
Sun-Dried Tomato and Vegetable Pizza, 82
Sun-Dried Tomato-Stuffed Mushrooms, 25
Sweet Cheese Crepes with Cherries Jubilee, 178
Sweet Potato Pancakes, 36
Swiss Chard Halibut with Ginger Sauce, 124

t

Tandoori Chicken, 99
Tasso and Spinach Pierogi, 165
Thai Steamed Mussels, 124
Tuscan Seafood Bake, 125

v

Veal Roulade with Caper Dressing, 140
Vegetable Frittata, 37
Vegetable Marinara, 154
Vegetable Orecchiette Soup, 69
Vegetables
  Black Bean-Stuffed Sweet Potatoes, 72
  Broiled Chiles Rellenos, 72
  Creole Stuffed Bell Peppers, 73
  Family-Style Ratatouille over Southern Corn Bread, 74
  Grilled Spring Vegetable Pizza, 74
  Grilled Tofu with Olive Tapenade and Preserved Lemons, 75
  Herbed Rice Cakes with Red Bean Sauce, 76

Heritage Shepherd's Pie, 77
Italian Vegetable Tart, 78
Mushroom and Artichoke Pasta, 78
Napa Cabbage and Mushroom Sauté, 79
Stir-Fried Rice Noodles, 80
Stuffed Peppers with Hominy Grits, 80
Summer Squash with Shaved Romano, 81
Sun-Dried Tomato and Vegetable Pizza, 82

Vegetarian Pesto Lasagna, 83
Vegetarian Pesto Lasagna, 83
Venison Marsala with Rosemary Sweet Potatoes and Onions, 141

W

Warm Spinach and Artichoke Dip, 26
Wild Mushroom Torte, 27

ABBREVIATIONS

STANDARD

tsp.	=	teaspoon
tbsp.	=	tablespoon
oz.	=	ounce
lb.	=	pound
doz.	=	dozen

METRIC

ml.	=	milliliter
l.	=	liter
g.	=	gram
kg.	=	kilogram
mg.	=	milligram

STANDARD METRIC APPROXIMATIONS

1/8 teaspoon	=	.6 milliliter		
1/4 teaspoon	=	1.2 milliliters		
1/2 teaspoon	=	2.5 milliliters		
1 teaspoon	=	5 milliliters		
1 tablespoon	=	15 milliliters		
4 tablespoons	=	1/4 cup	=	60 milliliters
8 tablespoons	=	1/2 cup	=	118 milliliters
16 tablespoons	=	1 cup	=	236 milliliters
2 cups	=	473 milliliters		
2 1/2 cups	=	563 milliliters		
4 cups	=	946 milliliters		
1 quart	=	4 cups	=	.94 liter

SOLID MEASUREMENTS

1/2 ounce	=	15 grams		
1 ounce	=	25 grams		
4 ounces	=	110 grams		
16 ounces	=	1 pound	=	454 grams